mean with money

mean with money

HUNTER DAVIES

POMONA

A POMONA BOOK P-010
Mad in England!

Published by Pomona 2005

1 3 5 7 9 8 6 4 2

Pomona Books
PO Box 50, Hebden Bridge, West Yorkshire HX7 8WA, England, UK
Telephone 01422 846900 · e-mail ursula@pomonauk.co.uk
www.pomonauk.co.uk

Distribution: Central Books Ltd., 99 Wallis Road, London E9 5LN
Telephone 0845 458 9911 · Fax 0845 458 9912
e-mail orders@centralbooks.com · www.centralbooks.com

Reps: Troika, United House, North Road, London N7 9DP
Telephone 020 7619 0800

A CIP catalogue record for this book
is available from the British Library

ISBN 1-904590-13-6

Set in 12 on 15.5 pt Granjon
Typeset by Christian Brett

Printed and bound by JW Arrowsmith Ltd., Bristol

CONTENTS

— £ —

Thanks to John Witherow, Naomi Caine
and William Kay of *The Sunday Times*
for their support, encouragement
and of course the cheques ...

INTRODUCTION

— £ —

The title was a mistake. It started off, my little column, being called *Me and My Money*, which was sensible and simple, inoffensive and ordinary enough but one day, after about a year, a new sub-editor misheard the title. He thought it was called *Mean with Money*. Say each one quickly — 'Me and My Money' and then 'Mean with Money' and you can understand the confusion.

First time it appeared in print, I rang up to complain, bloomin' cheek, what a liberty, it's not true, certainly not, no one is going to call me mean. Even if it's me doing the name calling. How shameful to appear to admit such a thing in public. I really was quite embarrassed. I'm not having that, so I thought. But everyone else thought it a very apt title. After all, isn't that what I have really been writing about all this time? Isn't it my recurring theme? So why not come out of the closet and confess?

I've now got used to it, faced up to the fact that it is true, more or less. Obviously I don't consider myself miserly and ungenerous, none of those nasty connotations which usually go hand in hand with meanness. What I don't like is spending money on unnecessary things, such as taxis. I sit in them with clenched fists and buttocks, willing lights to be green, the roads to be clear. And the prices, dear God, have you seen the prices recently? What I really hate, even more, is waste, hence I have always switched off lights, screamed at the kids if they went out of a room and left the telly on. I have gone through life eating up the rubbishy, soggy, mouldy, horrible fruit left in the bowl by everyone else, even though it tastes soggy and horrible. It costs money, you know, fruit doesn't grow on trees, so I told them. Okay don't be so clever, I know it does but money doesn't.

It turned out thousands, if not millions of other people are a bit like me, can identify with my petty meanesses, who also search out the best offers, hunt for little bargains, which of course turn out to be anything but. Most people at some times, at some stages, can be mean with money, so it began to appear, from all the correspondence and reaction. Which is not quite true. In my own home for example, my wife is the exact opposite. I have for a long time been well aware of what my family consider my shortcomings but which, ah ha, I see as virtues. Oh yes, someone has to think about money in this house, to organise savings, try to cut out waste.

Now I look back, I have always been interested in money. Not in a mean sense as I didn't have any to be mean with but in the sense of being highly aware of the need for it, carefully saving all my pennies as a paper boy till I could afford to pay a deposit on my Raleigh Lenton bike, green, racing handle bars, with Sturmey Archer gears. At one time, while still at school, I had three little jobs — newspapers, delivering groceries, helping on the Christmas post. I was obsessed by savings, for whatever I was saving for. My rationale was necessity. My father was an invalid throughout most of my childhood suffering from multiple sclerosis. There were no wages coming into the house so I never got any pocket money. I had to earn money if I wanted to have any, then once I'd got any I had to take good care what I spent it on. That's my excuse. But I know now it's not really environment and upbringing which makes us wholly like we are. Nature has just as much to do with it as nurture. It was how I was born, coming out canny.

Once I began to earn money, from my journalism and books, and eventually had a bit over at the end of the month, or the year, I looked around for sensible but safe investments, such as buying a country cottage or a bungalow for my Mum, keeping it in my name, knowing I'd get it back one day. Was that mean? Or thinking ahead? But despite the interest in money, I don't actually know anything about it, as a subject, as a speciality. I've never been into stocks and shares, not really, not seriously. I don't know all the words and terms which float around the Money pages of the newspapers. I have no idea if a bull market is good or bad news.

I don't actually like spending time on money, no more than is necessary. I see time spent on money, thinking about it, moving it around, as a waste of time when I could otherwise be, well, making money. I can't and could never give anyone advice or tips. If asked, I usually say keep it under the bed. I've always been suspicious of financial advisors, even when I had no finance and could have done with a bit of advice, if just to ignore it. I didn't understand their language. It all seemed so foreign and complicated. They never seem able to explain things in simple terms I could understand. Over the years, on the rare occasions I have been persuaded to go along with one of their suggestions, usually because they had a nice suit and spoke proper, or I wanted rid of them, I almost always regretted it later. Yes, and I am thinking of the Equitable Life.

So the point of these columns I have been doing every month in *The Sunday Times* since April 1999 is just to rabbit on, share my ordinary experiences and thoughts about me and my money with other ordinary people out there, who are perhaps thinking and feeling and getting furious in much the same way. I tell the truth about my own experiences. Well, up to a point, making nothing up, but perhaps not always stating the actual amount of money I put into say the Equitable. I don't want to be faced by my own stupidity or my wife to find out how daft I have been.

The book is for people interested in money but not the technical stuff, the stock market faffings around, the ups and downs you owe me half a crown, the FT index or the PFI ratios, whatever they are. And also for people amused by money, by their own stupidity and weaknesses when faced by the subject of money, what to spend it on, how to save it, how to rise above it.

When Pomona suggested publishing a little collection of the columns I hesitated, thinking that even for bedside or lavatory reading, they were, well, a bit thin. So with the help of one of my daughters, Caitlin, I have added some odd facts and figures, stories and anecdotes, quotations and observations, all about money, funny as much as informative. And yes, before you ask, I have paid her, a small sum, though really, when you think how I brung them all up, lavished so much on them all, you'd have thought they'd have rushed to help me for nothing. Kids, eh.

Anyway, it has amused me to put this little offering together, adding in a few extra elements, in the hope that it might prove enjoyable for ordinary folk interested in an ordinary way about money.

Hunter Davies
London, 2005

CHAPTER ONE

*On children, accountants, shares,
pensions, houses, banks, and
other pains and pleasures*

— £ —

WHY HAVEN'T MY KIDS GOT
THE MISER'S TOUCH?

Is there a money gene? Like a musical gene, an artistic gene, a football gene; not that I'm sure they exist, except in the minds of those without them. What I mean is an interest and skill with money. That definitely exists but can it be picked up through heredity or environment? It's a question I ask myself when I look at my three children, now grown-up—or at least pretending to be.

I have always taken care of all money matters in this house. When the tasks were divvied up, that's what I got, along with driving and gardening. My wife got cooking, cleaning, shopping—all the dreary ones. I got money because I must have been interested in it. She certainly isn't. Left to her own devices, she'd leave it all in the bank—and not even ask if there was any interest. She can't understand me fussing around, taking bits from here, bits from there, little investments all over the place, just to get the odd extra 0.1% interest. She says the hours of thought, moaning and groaning I put in are not worth it. She refuses all supermarket loyalty cards whereas I carry mine around in a barrow. And she always ignores 'two for the price of one' offers. I go mad when shop assistants point out deals to persuade her to have another one free, and my wife says no.

When shopping, the prices on the whole do not bother her. She decides instantly, does not look elsewhere but buys at once. I compare and contrast, trail around looking for those magic words—'special offer' or 'reduced'. On the rare occasion I do any household shopping, she gives me a list at the top of which she writes in capitals —'NO BARGAINS.' It's true that a lot of my bargains turn out to be rubbish, stuff I didn't really want, inferior goods that only I will use. Oh, the acres of soggy strawberries and putrid pears I have devoured over the years, all 'amazing value, not many left', which the children said yuk to and my wife wouldn't even put in the fruit bowl as they were health hazards.

I use second class stamps and ring after six if I can. I can be quite generous on biggish things, even spendthrift if it's really vital, such as a Caribbean holiday. But on piddling things, I count the pennies. So, two people, Jack Spratt and his dear wife, with two very different attitudes to money. With three children brought up in such a household, wouldn't you have expected one of them at least to be like me? Nope. No sign at all, not so far. They are clones of their generous mother, not their tightwad father. It used to drive me wild when one of them got a cheque for Christmas or a birthday, then either lost it or shoved it in a drawer and forgot it. When I get a cheque, however titchy, I walk straight to my nearest bank and put it in. I'm not sending it and losing two days' interest or, more likely, a week, using second class post. I like to see it physically going over the counter. They have always mocked me for doing this, saying what's the hurry, you're only saving pennies, how pathetic. And I say ah, look after the pennies and a Caribbean holiday will pay for itself. Eventually.

When I persuaded them all to open bank accounts, I found they were all using instant-access accounts, with minuscule rates. I tried to explain the advantages of a notice account, or term account, but they were all yawning by then. They considered it a waste of time when they only had a few pounds. I bought them all some premium bonds when they were young. At 18, I said, they would be able to look after them for themselves. I had imagined them not just keeping them but adding to them, having the fun of once a month winning

£50. Possibly, might be. Two immediately cashed them in and spent the money. The other lost them.

When the geneticists have stopped messing around with Dolly the sheep, I do hope they'll put their minds to humans. In my next life, I want to ensure that at least one of my children turns out interested in money. Otherwise, who is going to pay for me to go to Cobblers Cove in Barbados in my old age?

 It's a magical thing, money, when you think about it. A piece of printed coloured paper saying £20, 50 Euros or $100 or whatever, is in essence no different from a piece of coloured paper you might cut out of a glossy mag or newspaper. Yet one will enable you to pay bills, buy clothes, food, perhaps a large cappuccino but the other is pretty useless. Okay for lighting the fire, wrapping up your chips, but that's about all.

People will accept what we call and recognise today as money because they know other people will. But in the past, and at various stages in history, other objects have served as money. The Romans used salt as a form of currency. Cattle counted as money in many primitive cultures. American Indians used beads; cowrie shells were used in India; whales teeth among Fijians; stone discs on the Pacific island of Yap; tobacco among early American colonists and cigarettes and liquor in post Second World War Germany. Money, when you think about it, is all in the mind.

SHARE AND SHARES ALIKE

— £ —

I'm thinking of buying some Marks & Spencer shares. Possibly. Might be. Not because someone has tipped them, but I gather business is bad — could be the time to get in. So I looked at the share price, putting on my strongest glasses, and saw they were 389p. Hmmm, that seems low, but then what do I know? I've got Bonds, Tessas, National Savings certificates up to here — all at guaranteed rates. I don't go in for this variable nonsense, hence I've never fancied shares. I tell a lie. I bought £100 of Spurs shares in 1983 when they were launched — purely in order to frame them and put them on the wall along with my other Spurs memorabilia. I frame all the dividend cheques, average return £1.

I've bought other stuff for similar sentimental or dopey reasons. In 1986 I invested £3,000 in Playhouse Theatre shares, thinking I would become a luvvie. That awfully clever Jeffrey Archer was in the scheme. It collapsed almost at once. Not a penny, not even a penny back, did I ever get. I also invested £3,000 in the Groucho Club when it opened in 1984. Now that has been a brilliant investment. As a founder shareholder, I pay reduced fees and each year I get a massive return. I think it was £400 last year.

In 1987 I bought 100 Eurotunnel shares—price £350 —for each of my three children. I saw it as a patriotic gesture and an investment for their future. A free trip was thrown in, if the tunnel ever opened, if my children ever grew up. What a mistake. I try to forget about it, till more junk information arrives. I've been driven to screaming point by the acres of glossy paper and hefty envelopes that have thudded through the letterbox over the years. I never understood all the new issues, changes, proposals, all in two languages. Why do companies have to send all this stuff to every little investor and on such expensive paper? No wonder profits are so low. I've told my children they should keep the shares themselves, as they are in their names. No way, they said. Don't you dare give out our addresses. They don't want the junk mail. So now when Eurotunnel stuff comes in I bin it. I dare not even look at the share price.

I did once buy shares, purely to make money. In 1992 I interviewed Jim Slater the global investor. As I was leaving, I said come on Jim, give us a good tip. Betterware, he said. Buy Betterware at once. I bought 5,000 shares for £9,000. They did brilliantly. Six months later they were worth about double. Then life moved on, I forgot about them, till blow me, I woke up one day to find they were worth practically nothing. Jim had told me to sell them after six months, but I'd ignored that. When I did sell, I got only £5,000—practically half what I paid six years earlier. So it goes. That convinced me shares were not for me. I'm interested in money but not every day. Once a week is enough. Who is this woman Isa by the way? I've only just got to know Tessa, and now she's gorn.

Which reminds me. I wonder how the Marks shares are doing? Oh no. They've gone up to 410p since I last looked. Why didn't I buy at 389p? If I buy now, they'll probably go down again. I think I'll wait, for whatever it is I'm waiting for ...

 Metal used as money can be traced back to around 2,000 years before Christ but standardised metal coins, stamped with a ruler's or some authority's mark showing its appropriate weight and quality, were introduced by the ancient Greeks around 600 BC in Lydia, one of their states in Asia Minor, now part of Turkey.

When the system changed to the face value being what mattered rather than a coin's actual weight, it greatly helped commerce but lots of fiddles came in. People would shave bits off silver or gold coins, or even shake them in a bag in order to collect up any of the gold dust, hoping to pass off lighter coins by their face value. This was finally brought to a halt in the 17th Century when 'milling' was introduced, adding serrations round the edge of a coin. Any fiddles could then easily be detected. What a shame.

ACCOUNTANTS IN LEAGUE
WITH TAXMAN

— £ —

I've just spent the morning with Michael, my accountant. It's my annual morning with him, when he looks at
me sternly, tells me not to interrupt, we're coming to
that, why haven't you got your bank statement with you,
don't say you never kept those bills, must you have so
many little accounts, don't interrupt, I'll deal with that in
a minute.

I sit and look out of his window or examine his
framed certificates, as I have done for 15 years. I watch
him fill in my tax forms, waiting for the big news: how
much my wife and I have made this year and how much
tax we will have to pay. Today he gave me that news —
plus a bit extra I did not expect. I suppose not knowing
how much you've earned must seem strange to many
people. I've been a freelance now for 30 years and have
never known my income until the first week in May
when Michael tells me.

I did have another accountant for the first 15 years —
till we fell out. I had an unexpected tax bill and rang him
to ask what I should sell to pay it. He suggested a certain
investment, assuring me I would not incur capital-gains

tax. He was wrong: that year I'd already used my capital-gains allowance. I could easily have cashed in some National Savings Certificates instead. So I left him.

My present accountant gives no investment advice, just the facts, man, just the facts. He tots everything up, telling me the rules, what I am allowed and not allowed. I don't actually want investment advice such as tips about what to do with my money.

I did use a financial adviser about 10 years ago. What a mistake. He told me to take out a Capital Accumulator Plan with Norwich Union, which I did. The interest looked good on paper but the total didn't seem to grow. Then I realised that 23% had been taken off the first year and 5% a year ever after. I got out of it after seven years and was given £29,000 back for a £30,000 investment. Now I like to think if I make a mistake, it's my mistake. Most financial advisers, after all, turn out to be salesmen.

I would also like to live without an accountant. Not that I don't like Michael. I look upon him as a friend, know all about his life, his cars and we always have a jolly lunch after the tutorial is over and he has stopped bossing me around. It's just that I would like my affairs so organised, so simple, that they run themselves. I would, for example, like all my investments to be in National Savings, tax-free even if at low interest. Then I would never have to declare them or keep all that stupid paperwork.

But there is a conspiracy between the Inland Revenue

and the accounting profession. The Revenue brings in hundreds of new laws, rules, allowances and exceptions every year. Just when I think I am getting on top of them, know the funny words, got a grip on the weird logic and at last can understand what my accountant is on about, they go and change things yet again. The object is clearly to keep them all in work, off the streets and in their suits, sitting at their desks under their certificates.

Anyway, today my accountant gave me some rather deflating news. I thought I'd worked jolly hard this past year as a knockabout hack, doing a bit of this, a bit of that, shifting words all over the place, working on three books at various stages, plus a bit of BBC radio. I look upon the latter as charity work, as they pay so little. But for the third year running my wife has earned more than me. She just sits there, never rushing around, going nowhere, taking her time, never getting in a panic, writing only one book a year. What am I doing wrong?

Perhaps I will get a new accountant, one who is more creative and can arrange the figures so that I appear to be the man of the house (sorry, that just slipped out—I mean the main earner) once again.

Beer duty was initially introduced in 1643 to raise funds for the Civil War, later becoming a permanent excise tax.

Hearth tax was introduced in England, Ireland and Wales in 1662, with two shillings per hearth per year. It led to many a walled up chimney. It was repealed in 1689 but the Scottish Parliament introduced a hearth tax in 1691.

Land tax was introduced to England, Ireland and Wales in 1692.

Window tax was introduced in 1697. The amount depended on the number of windows in a house — e.g. four shillings for 10 to 20 windows, eight shillings for over 20 windows, etc. It led to many a walled up window (although 'blind windows' were also a Georgian housing design). Houses with fewer than eight windows became exempt in 1825. In 1851 the tax was abolished.

Income tax was introduced by the Tories in 1798 to support the war against France. The tax was repealed but reintroduced in 1803.

Value added tax was introduced in 1973.

Air passenger duty was introduced in 1994.

Climate change tax was introduced in 2001.

FIRST CLASS COLLECTION TURNS INTO
SECOND CLASS INVESTMENT

— £ —

I have made a big decision. I'm selling. All stock must go, everything must be cleared. They gave me such pleasure, provided years of illumination and amusement, apart from one appalling mistake which I am trying to forget, don't really want to talk about it—I must have been potty. What I am hoping is that by getting rid of my stamp stuff at a Sotheby's sale on July 16 I will expunge that blunder forever.

At the last count, looking in all cupboards, checking the shelves, lifting the carpets, I have 20 different types of collections. I began as an accumulator, going through life and throwing nothing away. One day you wake up and realise you have accumulated two similar items. You think: 'I know, I'll see if I can get another.' Once you acquire a third item, bingo, you are a collector. I did this with Prime Ministers. I found I had stashed away a letter from Harold Wilson and one from Ted Heath, both of whom I had once interviewed, for something or other, cannot remember what. I now have an autographed letter or item from every Prime Minister back to Robert Walpole in the 1720s. That collection is complete, in one sense, but still I add to it, getting better examples from junk stalls, collectors' fairs, auction sales.

Then there is my collection of suffragette material; that is now pretty good, as is my Beatrix Potter collection and my Beatles stuff. My collection of Lakeland post-cards is mostly tat but my 'number ones' do include several fine examples. By number ones I mean first editions of newspapers and magazines from the past 100 years. They include the *Daily Mail*, *Picture Post*, and *Private Eye*. Guess which is the most expensive? The *Eye*, by a long way.

It all started when I gave up Sunday football some 15 years ago. Life seemed so empty, so pointless. I could not bear to watch other people on the pitch on London's Hampstead Heath where I had played for 20 years, so I took to haunting stalls and fairs, looking for treasures.

One of the joys of having so many collections is that even on the crummiest stall or in the scruffiest junk shop, in the backest of beyond, you will always find something. You rush home, dead excited, only to find that you have it already.

My stamp collection spread itself down many alleys, from early Victorian stamps, American Columbus stamps, and a complete re-construction of a sheet of Penny Blacks. The latter took me 10 years, but oh what fun. I did not buy the stamps as an investment or think: 'This will go up in value.' I have mostly no idea what price I paid. Early on, I devised a code, scribbling it in pencil on the back so that my wife would not see how stupid I had been. Now I cannot understand the code, which is just as well.

The one and only time I did buy purely as an investment was in 1979. I had just begun to be interested in stamps, as a born-again collector, and at the time knew very little about them. I was persuaded by Stanley Gibbons, the famous stamp dealers, to buy a portfolio of stamps, which it would select, assuring me the values would rocket in a year, if not in a week, if not in minutes. At that time, stamp prices were rocketing. So I handed over a large sum for 10 little stamps, mainly Commonwealth issues, which I deposited at the Midland Bank at King's Cross, London. Okay then, I will tell you, but keep it quiet: I invested £4,000.

They must have seen me coming. About five years later, I had the stamps valued only to find that they were worth half what I had paid. Oh lor. So I kept them in the bank, waiting for good times. Now, 20 years later, Sotheby' has given them an estimated value of £1,500. If instead I'd bought a flat with that £4,000 it could well be worth about £100,000 today. What a fool. "It might have been worse," says Richard Ashton, head of stamps at Sotheby's. "I have widows coming in with stamps their husbands bought for £5,000 at around the same time as you and I have to tell them they'll be lucky to get £500."

At least the stamps I bought for my own amusement, the collections I later created, once I had a bit of knowledge, have almost all had modest increases in value. The moral is obvious: when it comes to collecting, buy what you like not what you think the market will like.

My reason for selling all the stamps is that I have not even looked at any of them for the past five years. So why keep them? I am going to spend every penny of the proceeds on one of my 20 collections I am passionate about—football memorabilia. Got any pre-war footie stuff to sell or swap? We accumulators have got to help each other.

China was the first country to start replacing metal money around AD 900, beginning with merchants in the great trading city of Chengdu. It reached Europe in the 18th and 19th centuries when it was styled by banks and governments as 'fiduciary' money, meaning the notes promised to pay the bearer the appropriate amount in silver and gold if required.

The Bank of England's Chief Cashier still makes a similar airy promise on all our notes. Next time you meet him, why not ask him to hand the dosh over in gold this time, if he doesn't mind, thank you very much.

TAKE MY ADVICE ON HOUSES —
I WISH I HAD

— £ —

Just been talking to a young couple, friends of ours, who have been out East where he's been working for Coca-Cola. I was on at them for years to buy a house in Blighty — get a stake before it's too late. Look, listen to your Uncle Hunt or that bloke in the Harry Enfield sketch. This is what you want to do. So they did.

They went after a rundown Victorian terrace house in London's Shepherd's Bush. The asking price was £230,000, which they offered, got accepted, only to be gazumped. Paid £260,000 in the end, feeling they'd been done; it was far too much. Why did they listen to Uncle Hunt? Last week, two years after they bought it, they had it valued and, you won't believe this, they were told it's now worth £440,000. Strewth. Why didn't I follow my own advice?

Damn lucky, of course. Buying into a street, a stone's throw from the Tube, five minutes before being gentrified by several upwardly mobile peoples who thought: 'Heh, this boring street isn't half bad, it will do us, for about half an hour, before we move and gentrify onwards and upwards.' And lucky that they arrived just as London prices generally began to shoot up.

The first property I bought with an investment view was in our own street. I didn't, of course, say that to my wife, the neighbours, even to myself. It was purely altruistic, to help my sister reside in London, wasn't it? Then when she moved on, it was for my dear old mum. She lived there for her last three years. Handy for us to look after her. Well, my wife to look after her—I was rushing around screaming, climbing on the roof to fix slates, trying to stop leaks, papering over cracks, botching up damp and disasters generally.

I bought it with one floor empty and two flats with sitting tenants. They were two old women and I never put their rents up, saying they could live there to the end of their days, which they did, happily. What they also did was ring me on the hour, day and night, about something or other. Every time I came home moaning and sobbing my wife said: "I've no sympathy, it's your own stupid fault, greedy capitalist pig."

Then our oldest and dearest went off to Sussex University. After one week in a very nice, modern, well-appointed student block, she said: "That's it, I'm leaving, can't stand all these students." She moved into a squat in Brighton. The day we went to see her we saw a rat coming out of the cooker. I have snaps of it somewhere. So I bought her a flat. Yes, Big Mick, flash git. How come, said my wife, that we went through our university days living purely on state grants, no family help at all? Ye olden days, I said. It's all changed. The state don't help no more. We'll have to pay for her rent, wherever she lives. This will save us plenty of money. I paid £18,000, I think. Awful to think I agonised and haggled and now cannot quite remember the price. One bed, kitchen and bathroom in a very nice Regency house in Bedford Square, right beside the West Pier—lovely situation, stunning views. She loved it and was very happy. So was her dear mama. And her papa, now a kind old flash git.

Then one day in 1987 we and the whole nation woke up to the worst hurricane in the modern history of England. In London we had a massive pear tree collapse in our back garden, just missing the house. In Brighton, the house containing the flat was totally wrecked. Yes, and I have snaps of that as well. Massive chimney stacks on the roof collapsed and fell through every floor of the house—amazing, freakish, very weird.

The whole house was empty for almost two years, for arguments and then rebuilding. Gawd, the aggravation it caused with insurance people, loss adjusters, management people, builders. I ended up with a pile of documents three feet high. And a daughter without a home. What a mistake. Yes, I did sell at a small profit in the end, which would have been more than sufficient to have made it all worthwhile but, dear God, the time and energy and stress.

Should I be mad enough to start such capers again, now another property boom is with us? Okay, don't shout at me, I'm not. But if I did then I would do two things. Buy anonymously, in a street far away, making sure no one knows my number. Get agents to do all the dirty work, even if they do take a whopping percentage. All the same, children, my advice is, was and ever shall be: buy property. You know it makes sense.

Dosh is one of the most popular terms for money in the UK today and common slang in Australia too. May come from the term 'doss-house', a cheap hostel/room, with dosh (from doss) meaning enough to pay for a bed for the night. Dosh was first recorded in 1914, meaning 'a bivvy; a temporary shelter or tent'. It wasn't until the mid-1940s that it began to mean money. On the other hand, it may be a mix of DOllars and caSH, which would suggest an American origin. It could also be derived from 'dash' which is alternatively described as an old African colonial term meaning a tip or bribe, or a word deriving from the West Africa term dashee. I hope that's clear.

Spondoolicks originated in the USA in the 1850s. It was out of use by the 1960s but revived in the 1980s. It comes from the Greek term 'spondylikos', a reference to a seashell which may have been used as currency.

Cash derived from an Indian word meaning compressed tea, once used as currency.

I'VE GOT MONEY TO BURN BUT I'M HANGING ON TO IT

— £ —

Are you rich? Come on, admit it. I've been calling myself rich for oh, decades now. I think I first spotted my state of richness about 20 years ago. I was coming back from a cheapo package holiday to the Algarve and to my own amazement, I did not buy a bottle of duty free.

I'd got my money out, was clutching my boarding card, comparing the prices, examining the labels, looking for special offers. 'I'll get a malt,' I thought. 'If I'm saving so much, I might as well go for something good for a change. But I don't really like malt.' By which time my brows were furrowed and my head aching. That's when the sky opened. And a voice in my head spoke. 'Don't be stupid, Hunt. Do you really want to cart this bottle all the way to Gatwick in order to save tuppence when you can well afford to pay full price on all the bottles of whisky you are ever likely to drink?' And I haven't done so for 20 years now.

That was a seminal moment, but I always did consider myself rich, as opposed to poor, the moment I started working. I hate those middle-class types who moan all the time about lack of money, saying they'll be on bread and water soon, boast boast, yet are paying a fortune on school fees, skiing hols and country cottages. I have always gone the other way, telling everyone how much I've got. As an employed person, I always told my colleagues my wage, just to annoy the management. Their plot, when they give a little rise, is to con everyone by telling them to keep it secret.

Some people mark their state of richness by the first time they started taking taxis without thinking. I won't ever reach that stage. I always think about it, then hold back. It's the clock clicking away when the cab's stationary—that's what gets me, ticking away my money. "I'll just get out here," I say. "This is where I live." Very often I'm still miles away.

'I'll have it, whatever the price.' People remember the first time they said that phrase, ordinary people, who can't really afford it, as well as millionaires.

David Beckham and Gary Neville were wandering round Manchester one day, window shopping, wondering what to do with their spare millions, when Becks said: "Go on, buy that £8,500 Rolex watch." Gary was appalled by the price, refusing to spend that sort of money. "Go on, live a little," said Becks. "Certainly not," said Gary. "Anyway I don't wear a watch."

I'm with Gary. I just couldn't spend that sort of money, even though in theory I could. But I often do look in shop windows, auction catalogues, car sales and think: 'I can afford that'. And do nothing about it. I just like the feeling.

I interviewed a lottery millionaire once whose cross in life had been his old beat-up car. If he ever won the lottery, so he promised himself, he'd have a Jaguar. Six months later, he was still driving his old car. As flash cars sped past him, he got great pleasure in thinking: 'Yeah, I could buy one of those, but I don't want to now.' In his case, his fantasy had become realisable, so it was no longer a fantasy. In my case, well, I could never spend money on a flash car. Yes, I do have a Jaguar, but it cost me £10,000 and is five years old. When I think of those six dopey Man United lads who have each spent £150,000 on a Ferrari I have to lie down.

We are all stuck with our own personality. We can't alter it, whether we are richish or poorish, which means you get mean millionaires and flash ones. If I have £1,000 to invest, I look at all the options, comparing fractions of percentages, worrying about the best deals, when there's so little in it. I know I'd be just the same with a million to spare, or a billion. In fact I feel sorry for those with big wads, as the worry about what to do with it must be worse.

And yet when I do lash out, overcome my natural tightness and meanness, and spend my money on some self-indulgence, something strange happens. I bought four fields round our Lakeland home, daft really. I haggled and havered, fussed and fretted and now, just five years later, I can't remember what I paid. So I need not have spent so much time getting the price down.

Forgetting the price is a sign of three things. First, a lousy memory. Second, it can also be a matter of blanking it out, because of guilt, or having been stupid. Or, third, simply through being rich. Which I am. In my mind, anyway.

Hetty Green is known for being the richest American woman ever—and one of the most tight-fisted. She was born in 1834 to a wealthy whaling family in Massachusetts and at a young age she took a keen interest in business. She read the financial pages to her father at the age of six and by 13 was working as a bookkeeper in the family business. When her father died she inherited a fortune and continued to make more. And save more. On her 21st birthday she refused to light the candles on her cake, so she could return them to the shop the next day for a refund. She spent half the night looking for a lost two-cent stamp, bought broken biscuits in bulk, and for lunch ate dry oatmeal warmed on an office radiator. Overall her philosophy was 'Buy cheap and sell dear' and much of her income came from money lending. When she died in 1916 —apparently after quarrelling with a maid about the price of skimmed milk—her fortune was $100 million. A museum in New Bedford was recently opened in her memory, to celebrate her financial wizardry.

BANKING ON BANKS

— £ —

What are banks for? I mean physical banks, bricks and mortar, polished wood and marble banks. The ones that sit there looking smug in the High Street. Their end is nigh, now that they are eating up each other. But they have already become pretty pointless and a waste of space in recent years.

A hundred years ago I could see the purpose, when every little town had about 10 different banks, all competing, all trying to look impressive and imposing. And they needed space inside for people to lug in their bags of copper and silver and have it counted. Now we get paid by cheque or straight into the bank. And to get cash out, we use the cash machines. So what's the point? I say 10 banks in every little town because I have a collection of cheques from dead Carlisle banks and that's how many I've got. Can't remember why I started. Dopey, really. I have one from the Carlisle Commercial Bank, dated 1837, that's really good, and one from Joseph Monkhouse's Bank, 1858. Both have rather pretty vignettes. Lovely lettering.

I also started a collection of celebrity cheques, as signed by famous people, which I thought was a brilliant idea, but I've only got one so far: Somerset Maugham.

Nationally, I think there must have been about 4,000 banks at one time, most, including Barclays and Lloyds, established by Quakers. Now we are down to just a handful. Gobble gobble. Is that another one going?

I joined the Midland 40 years ago when I got the first payment on my student grant. Because it came on a Midland Bank cheque, I thought I had to take it there. I just never left. I once tried to. I had my account at the Midland at King's Cross in London because I worked near there at the time. Then I started working from home. It became so inconvenient, and parking was hell, so I wrote to say I was transferring. The manager had me in and said, 'don't leave, please, we'll pay your parking fines.' It rather endeared me to him. I did leave, but for another branch of the Midland in Hampstead. I feel at home there, having watched the staff grow out of nappies.

And yet I haven't been in for six months. That's because we are at present in Lakeland where we now live six months each year. From here, I post my cheques. When I'm back in London, I'll be going in all the time. I like the act of personally taking in my cheques, even the titchiest, and seeing the smiles on their faces (joke). My wife can't understand. Oh come on, pet, I say, if I post a £50 cheque, I can lose three days' interest, but by dashing across I save, hold on, let me count—it must be easily 2p.

We have a joint account, always have had, though her right-on chums say 'how can you, what sort of feminist are you?' I say to her 'sign here' and I could be off to Barbados with the lot for all she knows. She wouldn't know a cash machine if she met it in her porridge. She has a PIN number, which I got for her, but thinks it's something to do with sewing or knitting. I love cash-points. I really do. I often go twice a day. Not to get money out but to fondle the little slips, see the latest state of my balance. Yes, I know they don't change in a day, but it amuses me. What else have I got to do?

My children think I'm potty. I tell them it's much more fun than the stupid old internet or any boring old computer game. Easy to use, doesn't cost anything. Oh gawd, I hope it doesn't. Behind your back, these high street banks do pull a few tricks—and make terrible mistakes. I caught them once sending the same sum twice to the Equitable. Took weeks to sort out, but I spotted it, went in and duffed them up. That's one advantage of a bank on the high street.

I'll miss them when they go. Money is so abstract, especially today, so the physical feel of a bank is reassuring. I like to look at the tellers behind, ever so earnest, ever so self-important, lips pursed. I observe their hairstyles, that unfortunate tie, and think yes, they are real people, so my money must be real. Then I wonder where they keep it. No doubt the odd bank will remain, a door in a side street with one teller to take in hard cash, though by then only drug dealers will be lugging in their coppers.

What will happen to banks? They do make excellent restaurants or wine bars, as many have already become, all that polished wood and marble looks classy. Or perhaps museums of banking. One in every town to remind us of ye olden days. My 10 dead bank cheques are framed in the hall at present, but I wouldn't mind contributing them to the first museum. I do like to help.

 Credit cards: a small card, usually plastic, with some sort of identification on it, which allows you to charge goods or services to your account. Or someone else's if you've managed to nick it and also got the secret PIN number.

The use and abuse of such cards began in the USA in the 1920s when firms such as hotels or oil companies began issuing them to regular customers for use at their company outlet.

Universal credit cards, which could be used at a variety of establishments, not owned by the same company, was introduced by Diners Club in the USA in 1950, originally aimed at people using restaurants. The card holder paid an annual fee and was billed on a monthly basis. The firms and establishments co-operating paid a service charge of around 5% of the total billing.

Debit cards were a later innovation, begun by the Bank of America in California in 1959, whereby the banks themselves issued cards to customers. Customers don't pay a fee, but their accounts are charged at once. The firms involved do pay a percentage but at least they get their payments promptly.

I'M COUNTING THE COST
OF SAVING

— £ —

I think I'm going off money. It's all too confusing, too time consuming, too annoying. Worst of all, it can be so expensive, worrying about money. It's months ago now since my accountant told me how much my wife and I could put into our pension fund this year. I don't actually have a pension fund, as such. I cashed it in last year after I woke up one morning and let out a huge scream: I'VE BEEN CONNED!

Well, I'd conned myself. I hadn't realised you never get it back. Your capital has gone forever, your hard-earned savings lump, the moment you put it in a pension fund. They own it. You don't, not any more. That had never struck me. My foolishness. Then when I saw how low the annuity rate had dropped, I realised I'd be lucky to get any half-decent returns back, unless I started taking it now and then lived to be 159.

Which of course I intend to do. Oh yes. That'll teach Equitable Life a lesson. The annuity rates are now a bit better, which is something, but still the only attraction of a pension fund I can see is the tax relief you get by paying into it—I have saved 40% income tax on the money

I put in. My accountant is all for this, as accountants are. It's how they're brought up, comes with their mother's milk. "Paying less tax is good for you, Michael," they're told. "Always remember that." But in this case, it's not necessarily so.

You should see the backs of envelopes, sides of news-papers, and even whole notebooks I have filled with my little figures. If I pay tax on a notional £10,000 I have only £6,000 to invest, but you can safely get 7.15% in Northern Rock at present and still have your £6,000. If I live 10 years, or 20 years, would I be better off putting the whole £10,000 in a pension scheme? Don't try to work it out. You'll just give yourself a headache. It's a nonsense, really, that something negative—not paying the tax—should be the main attraction. All the same, I asked Equitable Life for a quote.

While they got out their *Oxford Dictionary of Quotations*, I saw lots of ads from Legal & General, boasting about its pensions. I rang the number. It only took three weeks to get a human being to talk to me. All I wanted to know was if their annuity rates were better than Equitable's. Guess what? They said: "Go away, you silly person." They wouldn't take my money. Something to do with the fact that I was going to cash in my pension and take the annuity at once. They would have to charge and it wouldn't be worth it.

I then contacted Friends Provident. The problem here was stopping a rep coming to my front door on the next

Tube. And I was in the Lake District at the time. Just give me the facts, man. It did eventually, and the rates were not as good as Equitable's. All that faffing around. So I had a lie down, only to be disturbed by BT offering me marvellous savings if I did something or other. I haven't even got the hang of Family and Friends yet. It keeps sending me lists of telephone numbers I never recognise, friends I never knew I had. Where do they come from—central casting? Actors hired to swear blind they know you.

I studied the guff carefully, persuaded that I really would save myself if I changed to thingy call. I could be pennies in. Then there was a knock at the door. The electricity board trying to sell me gas. Some mistake surely. "No sir, just compare these figures, look at these offers," he said. Which of course you can't. When you try, you find that like is not being compared with like. But I tried, oh I tried. I elected myself in charge of the finances in this house, one likes to be responsible. I thought long and hard for a week, closed both eyes, signed some forms, all in a foreign language and very small print. Then I rewarded myself by switching on the telly to find that Chelsea v Man Utd was not on Sky, for which I pay a subscription. It was on Ondigital, whatever that is. Should I change? It'll mean sitting down with notebooks, sucking more pencils, comparing and contrasting the differing and bewildering offers and deals to find the best price for what I think I want.

So I went to bed early. In my head I tried to tot up the weeks and hours, the time and energy I had put in to trying save money on money. If only I had spent that same amount of time working, I would have made money, far more than I'll possibly save.

If you think about it, thinking about money is a waste of money. I offer that quote to the *Oxford Dictionary*. For no charge.

"Business, you know, may bring money,
but friendship hardly ever does."
– Jane Austen

"The rule is not to talk about money with people
who have much more or much less than you."
– Katharine Whitehorn

CUTTING THE COST OF CALLS
TO BOTTYLAND

— £ —

We have a daughter who lives in Botswana, on the edge of the Okavango Delta, right beside a river full of crocodiles, 900 miles from the main town, thatched roof on the little rondavel where she works. You've got the picture. Except she has a satellite phone, satellite television, state-of-the-art computer, internet and all that stuff, most of which we haven't got here in so-called civilisation. I'm typing this on an Amstrad PCW, about a hundred years old, which is going to the Victoria & Albert Museum when I finish with it. This could be soon, such as at the end of this piece.

My daughter is always moaning that we haven't got e-mail, whatever that is. But we do write and fax all the time and once a week, on a Saturday morning, we ring her for long chats. Well, my chats are not so long, when it's my turn, as I'm watching the clock, being a mean beggar. But my dear wife, she can rabbit on until it's almost Sunday morning. She came off the phone the other Saturday, after 40 minutes, with the phone steaming, and said: "Hmm, that was a good chat." Do you realise, I said, that your load of old chat has cost me, sorry us, because she does earn more than me and gets ratty if I go on about my money instead of our money — do you realise that cost £40?

"Heh, that's cheap," she said. "All that way, 10,000 miles. Amazing. Yet I could hear her, clear as anything. Isn't science wonderful? It's a bargain, at £40, if you ask me. I'll ring her even longer next week ..."

I had to sit down for a bit, as I had begun to steam as well. Then I started ringing round, looking for cheapo phone calls. I tried to stop thinking how the pursuit of anything, from car insurance, air flights to cups of tea or packets of Strepsils, can take over your life, leaving you no time for anything else, such as living. Cups of tea, by the way, are £1 at Spurs, 60p at Arsenal. Yes, I agree, it's shocking. As for Strepsils, don't try Boots. I then remembered all the adverts for cheap phone calls. You must have seen them. They've been going for some time. I haven't quite understood them, but suddenly there's an avalanche, in all the newspapers, offering amazing bargains.

They boast calls as cheap as 2p a minute, usually for places I never ring, such as America, Australia and Ireland. Those are presumably popular places, because so many folks in Britain have relations or friends out there. I've never seen any special offers saying, Hurry Hurry, Cheapo Calls to Bottyland. (That's what we call Botswana. Behind its back, of course). I wasn't exaggerating when I told my dear wife that her 40 minute call had cost £40. BT's cheapest weekend rate to Botswana is 98p a minute. Weekdays it's a phenomenal £1.31. Don't tell me that's a bargain. I call it appalling.

So I rang something called First Telecom. Their rate for Bottyland is 76p a minute. Not bad, but it hardly seemed worth changing for that. I then rang Alpha Telecom and their rate is 40p. I said: "Heh, I'll have some of that. What's the catch?" No catch. There's no joining fee, no subscriptions. You use your existing BT phone, just add a special number at the beginning each time you ring. You pay in advance, a minimum of £15. So I did, dubiously giving them my Visa card number.

I was worried there might be a catch or a trick, that the voice at the other end might at this moment be jetting off to Barbados having run up thousands of pounds on my Visa bill. But last Saturday it worked. No probs. My wife had a 38 minute call for only £15. Now that is a bargain. I felt well pleased — until this morning. I saw yet another advert from yet another telephone firm: Planet Talk. Don't they all have poncey, pretentious names? I bet it's probably a man and a boy, sitting in a telephone box. Or is it Kevin Maxwell, sitting on a yacht? I heard him interviewed on the radio last week and he appears to be about to make a fortune on these cheapo telephone systems.

Apparently, you rent certain lines across the world, for a certain amount, which is the same thing that BT does. Then it's up to you to fill them, or rent them on, or do something equally clever to make a lot of money quickly without actually doing much or producing anything at all. Weird, isn't it, being able to buy and sell time?

Anyway, Planet Talk's rate for Botswana turned out to be only 20p per minute. Oh no. If only I'd found them first, before I paid money in advance to the other firm. But not much. I'll switch from them to the cheaper one. But how long can this go on? I could be sitting here, on the phone all day, ringing each new firm that advertises a lower rate, then another firm with an even lower rate. I can see it now. I'm sure that way a sort of madness lies. I've probably wasted about £40 this week in time spent ringing these firms when I could have been working. Not that I'm telling my wife that.

 When Joseph Leek, a 90 year old man who 'lived like a pauper' died in Hull in 2003 his family were amazed to find out he was a millionaire. Joseph Leek left £1.1 million to the Guide Dogs for the Blind Association, and nothing to his two daughters. His money-saving schemes were said to include watching TV at a neighbour's house to save on bills and dressing in second-hand clothes. Press reports said Leek, 'would not spend money on items he considered unnecessary'.

CHAPTER TWO

Sun specs, teeth, personalised numbers, and a taxman calls

— £ —

I'M FLYING CONCORDE —
ON THE CHEAP OF COURSE

I always go for bargains, the cheapest. My wife is the opposite. 'No special offers', is her mantra. And I hate waste. As you know, when there's a bowl of fruit on the table, and we have them all the time, being very posh, even when nobody is ill, I always feel every one, which makes my wife scream—before taking the baddest, squashiest, nastiest. I have gone through much of my life doing all this because I know my family would never ever soil their dainty lips or tums with anything remotely orf. So who will eat them? Moi. Even if I do get the runs. I don't think I've eaten a perfect orange, apple or pear since, hmm, Mafeking.

But I do have one indulgence, when I don't worry about waste or cost. Every January since 1986 we have gone to the West Indies, starting at Cobblers' Cove in Barbados, then wandering round the islands. Costs a packet but what the hell, it's my annual time off from being a cheapskate. I don't plan to leave my children any money. They've had enough advantages in life, such as being my children. We always go just after my birthday, January 7, the end of the most expensive season of the year, the Christmas and New Year hols. After that, prices come down a bit, if only marginally. Still a lot of money. Every year I moan about the cost of the flights. Yet guess what I have gone and done?

I was speaking to our travel organiser, Elegant Resorts in Chester, and I said: "By the way, I see there's a Concorde flight to Barbados on the same day we have booked to go in Club." We always go Club Class to the West Indies. My wife insists. She wouldn't go otherwise. Rather stay at home and see if the dishwasher has still got a leak, which it has — don't talk about it. We'll leave our housesitters to deal with that.

For a seven-day stay at Cobblers' Cove, half board, there and back by Club, the price is £3,645 each. By upgrading to Concorde, one way, the price is £4,530. A jump of £885, but not a lot, really, to fly on an icon. And a total snip when you think that the scheduled British Airways Concorde return to Barbados, if you had to walk in off the street or trawl through the net and buy a ticket, is £5,970. Flight only. So before I could stop myself, I heard a voice, very like mine, saying: "Okay then, I'll have some of that. If there are two seats available on Concorde that day." And there were. I didn't tell my wife until last week, on New Year's Day. Her millennium present. I do spoil her.

"You'll never believe this," I said. "But you know we're going this Sunday on BA273 departing at 8.40 in the morning. Well, we should be there around the time we leave."

"What have you been drinking?" she said. "I thought that cooking sherry was finished."

"The time difference is four hours, pet, and Concorde flies in four hours. We should be there by nine o'clock, in time for two breakfasts."

"Concorde!"

"Yes, dear. I knew you'd be pleased."

"I am not. What a stupid waste of money. I much prefer Club. Far more space and leg room in Club. And I don't mind eight hours, if it's a day flight."

Notice she didn't ask how much extra it was. Being a person who never penny pinches, this wouldn't come into her pretty head.

"You of all people. What on earth made you do it?"

"Dunno. Something came over me. A sort of funny turn. Just thought I'd surprise you, and myself. Don't want to be typecast for ever as a tightwad."

"Showing off," she said.

"To whom? Don't be silly. It's a new millennium, innit. Let's celebrate."

But don't worry, I won't be doing it again, not for another 1,000 years. So if you are on Concorde today, look out for me. Seats 17A and 17B.

The wealthy eighth Earl of Bridgewater knew how to treat his canine friends — 11 of them sat down with Francis Henry Egerton each day to eat dinner off silver plates. Each dog had a napkin and a servant hovering behind each chair. The dogs all had leather boots. The Earl (b. 1756) was a boot lover too. He wore different footwear each day and then used the discarded pairs as a calendar, setting them in rows around his house.

MAKING A SPECTACLE OF MYSELF

— £ —

I would like to share a tip with you. Not to tip a share with you. What do I know about shares, gilts, the FTSE top how'syourfather and other nonsense? I did once know what a p/e ratio was, as my old gym master told me. But now I've forgotten.

My tip is how to save yourself some money, should the same thing happen to you as has just happened to me. While having a swim in Barbados, on my January holidays, a huge wave raced off with my sun specs. Don't ask why I was wearing sun specs in the sea. How stupid. What a poseur, especially as it was pouring down, black clouds, couldn't see a thing anyway. It does chuck it down in the West Indies, often for 40 seconds at a time. That's one of the pleasures. That's why it's so green.

I was furious as they were my only pair of sun specs, a prescription pair as well. I had to peer for the rest of the holiday, my eyes screwed up, and at my age, one can't afford too much eye screwing. The bags, my dears, the bags. I'm long sighted, or is it short sighted? I never know the difference, like I can never remember if pm or am is morning.

I use specs for driving, going to football matches, anything far away, such as more than 10 yards. Reading, I'm okay for. But not for walking around the planet. So last week, on my return home, I went to Dollond & Aitchison, the shop where I'd bought my specs, and asked how much another pair would be. There was a lot of whizzing on the computer and screen gazing. Why can't they just have a simple printed list they can look up? The answer was £88.99. Good golly, Ms Molly. I could buy a car for that. Ah, but if I bought another pair at the same time, the second pair would be only £20.

The world is stiff with these special offers, new deals, extra inducements, all complicated to work out, difficult to compare with elsewhere — and usually offering something you didn't come in for. I only wanted one pair, thank you. But then, I thought, a bargain is a bargain. So I said I'd think about it. Which meant I immediately rang our local cheapo cut-price specs shop, Betterspecs in Kentish Town. Its price was £88.99. What a coincidence. How do these great brains arrive at the same price, to a penny? Must be psychic. But no, they were not offering extra pairs cheaper or any other special offers.

So I went back to Dollond & Aitchison, said okay, you win. More whirling of the screen and the price was now £108.99. Bloody hell. I only came in yesterday. Talk about inflation. I called for the manager and after a lot of faffing on their side, huffing and puffing on my side, it turned out their £89.99 price quoted the day before was for the type of specs I'd had last time, which they now didn't have in stock. Hence they were now quoting me the next cheapest, £108.99. (Don't bother following these figures too carefully if they are hurting your eyes. I know exactly how you feel. I'm getting to the good bit in a moment. Honest. Just hang on a little bit longer.) I stormed out, vowing never to stumble over the doorstep again.

I was sitting that evening at home, watching football on TV, as I do every night, sometimes all day, plus weekends. I couldn't find my best pair of watching-television specs, so I put on an old pair. I have about three old pairs, with marginally different prescriptions, but I can wear them all, no bother, if I can't find my best pair. When into my head came this amazingly brilliant thought: what if I painted them? Surely prescription sunglasses are just prescription glasses dipped in some brown stuff or other? I could try that old tin of Ronseal under the stairs, if it's not gone all gungy or rock hard. Might smell a bit, stick to my bonce or my eyebrows, but quite obviously worth a try. If I've thought of this wheeze, perhaps those great brains of the specs industry have already cottoned on to it?

I'm now blanking Dollond & Aitchison, forever, so I rang Betterspecs. Bring the old pair in, they said. It will depend on whether they are too worn. In one hour, while I had a coffee at the Renoir caff nearby, they had dipped and dried my old specs — and they are absolutely, totally, excellent. Far better than the new pair I was going to get at £108.99. They have a more expensive frame for a start. And guess how much I was charged? Only £10. I had therefore saved myself almost £100. Yippee.

I might have saved even more if I had claimed on my holiday insurance for the lost pair, but that would have taken weeks of form filling, messing around, then they'd probably say go away, haven't you read the small print, are you blind or something? So, I pass on this tip for free. Please use it. I'd hate to see the specs industry making any more profit than it really, truly deserves.

All week I've been going round beaming. Quite easy to spot me. I'm the funny looking bloke walking up and down Kentish Town High Road in the middle of February wearing very dark sun specs.

The Sunday Times' list of the UK's richest people is based on estimates of the minimum wealth of Britain's 1,000 richest people or families. It includes people who are not British citizens but who live and work in Britain, and British citizens abroad. It doesn't include Rupert Murdoch, who in theory would be number four on the list, because he's an American citizen and is based in the US. Among those on the list, around 247 inherited their wealth, including 63 aristocrats.

1. Roman Abramovich   £7500m
   oil, football, investments

2. The Duke of Westminster   £5,000m
   property

3. Hans Rausing and family   £4,950m
   food packaging

4. Philip Green   £3,610m
   retailing

5. Lakshmi Mittal   £3500m
   steel

6. Sir Richard Branson   £2600m
   transport, mobile phones

7. Kirsten and Jorn Rausing   £2575m
   inheritance, bloodstock, investment

8. Bernie and Slavica Ecclestone   £2323m
   motor racing

9. Charlene and Michel de Carvahlo   £2260m
   inheritance, brewing, banking

10. David and Simon Reuben   £2200m
    property, metal trading

RICH THOUGHTS

— £ —

Did you read about that 17-year-old internet whizz-kid who created a £45m company in his bedroom? YaBoo it's called. He provides essays for students all round the world, on any subject, in any language. All you do is feed in a page of your own writing, in your own style and it comes out as if you have written it. Amazing.

He has a good middle-class background, as most of these whizzes have. His mother is professor of sheep studies at Carlisle University and his dad was Bishop of Cockermouth. His next venture is to edit the internet. As we all know, it's sewage in, sewage out, so the first person to successfully edit all the rubbish before it comes out, will clean up.

He has made a bid for Sellafield, which the government is backing — what else can it do with the plant? And he has hired 3,000 sub-editors who will move in soon to begin programming. This should make him about £2 billion. And he hasn't even started shaving. Incredible.

If you haven't heard of him, it may be because I made him up. But I bet for a moment you felt pangs of jealousy that you, or your children, or someone, anyone, wasn't in your back bedroom making millions of pounds on an internet scheme. Envy of other people's money is natural, if not logical. I have just given up subscribing to The Bookseller after more than 20 years. I just couldn't bear to read any more stories of authors I have never heard of being given advances of £1m or so for silly-sounding books they still haven't written. For my own silly books, the biggest advance I ever had was £35,000. For the next one, due out next month, I got only £10,000. It's a book I really, really wanted to do, so I was happy with the deal, but not happy when I read what others are supposedly getting.

Yet, on the other hand, I don't feel jealousy towards Richard Littlejohn, our best-paid hack who is reportedly on £850,000 a year. I think, go to it Rich, screw the beggars for as much as you can get.

House prices are the other subject making people feel bitter and twisted. There is a street in London's Hampstead called Downshire Hill that I often walk down and think, yeah, that was the one I could have got for £20,000. We looked at three once when we were thinking of moving, but never did. Now they are worth, no it's too obscene to mention. You will only be sick, especially if you are the retired Bishop of Cockermouth, living in a sheep shelter.

Last week I had lunch with a friend who over the years has bought and converted properties. He told me about one that was full of tenants when he bought it, dirt cheap. Now it's empty and worth, oh, another obscene amount. Strangely enough, I felt no pangs of jealousy. I just thought of all the aggravation he must have had, repairs needing to be done and people moaning constantly. If it's not your field of activity, then it's harder to summon up blind, furious, naked jealousy.

But we are living in a time when it's easy to feel mild envy when we hear of all these instant, easy millions. We know it will end in tears as it did with the railway boom of the 1840s, but we can't help thinking, why didn't we get in there before the crying started? So the first thing to remember — if you have missed the boat, friends — is that the rich are like us, only richer. That's about it. No, I didn't get that from a Christmas cracker. I got it from life, as it happens.

I have interviewed or met scores of millionaires over the years, from moguls to lottery winners, pop stars to footballers, and almost all are bugged by something or someone, can feel jealous and bitter, insecure, depressed and think they are not rated. Just like the rest of us. Sir Paul McCartney is not at all pleased when he performs his song Yesterday - the royalties go elsewhere, all because certain rights were sold years ago. For years, Sir Richard Branson's failure to beat Camelot for the lottery franchise has been niggling him.

The second thing to tell yourself is that so many of the self-made are a bit unbalanced, even weird, over-compensating for certain personality disorders. Third,

you should always remember that you will still be you—
with your own weaknesses and personality.

Feel better? Well, I'm trying to cheer you up. And
myself for that matter. For I just know I would be even
happier with that million pound book contract and a
house in Downshire Hill.

John F Kennedy, while campaigning for the 1960 Democratic
presidential nomination, visited a coal mine in West Virginia.

"Is it true you're the son of one of our wealthiest men?"
asked an old grizzled miner. JFK admitted it was true.

"And you've never wanted for anything?"

JFK nodded his head.

"And is it correct that you've never done a day's work with
your hands in your life?"

"I guess so," said Kennedy.

"In that case, let me tell you something," said the miner.
"You ain't missed nothing."

MONEY ISN'T THE ROOT OF ALL EVIL
— MY TEETH ARE

— £ —

There are two things I dislike spending money on. Well, more than two, but I don't have the space. The two are connected because they are basically maintenance charges, costs you can't get out of, but don't seem to constitute an improvement or give added value.

The house is the first and obvious one. I hate having to mend things, put in new floors when they rot, replace ceilings when they collapse. You spend all that extra money and what do you end up with? What you started with. Now adding a garage, if you haven't had one, that's different. I didn't mind spending a fortune when we put a garage in our London home. They do increase the value of any property. I'd now love a conservatory, but she won't let me have one, the rotter. "Get that roof fixed first," she says, "And the floor where we had the flood, before you start thinking of stupid additions."

The other thing I hate spending money on is me. Just like the house, my body is at the stage where things are falling to pieces and the rot is setting in. It will put you off your porridge to hear about my poorly toe, but that's all right at present. What's not okay is my teeth. I've gone through life with good teeth. A bit uneven, but that never worried me, not since a primary school teacher told me that uneven teeth are attractive. So, no problems apart from the odd filling — until a few months ago. I got awful pains which the dentist said would need root-canal treatment. And I'd also need a crown, so he said.

I am awfully brave, always have been, being a man, but being treated like royalty for having a bit of dental treatment, that did seem a bit excessive. He's a very nice dentist, a New Zealander, very gentle, had him for 20 years. He explained that a crown is a sort of pretend tooth, which is fixed over the dodgy one after the root work has been done. And how much will that be, squire? He thought hard and said: "Well, it will be £300 for the root-canal treatment, then £650 for the crown. So you're looking at £1,000." I said: "I'm looking at the door. Then I'll be looking for someone to do it free on the national health." Too late, it turns out, by several decades. The NHS now hardly exists in dentistry. Almost everyone pays for almost everything. In that case, why not just yank the blessed tooth out? I don't mind a gap. "We don't take teeth out," he said. He then gave me a lecture on the perils of leaving a gap.

This crown thing then, what's it made of, gold or what? Yes actually, plus some platinum and a porcelain bond. In that case I'll have a cheapo job, make me one out of plastic. It's at the back, so who cares what it looks like? More lectures while he explained what a delicate, technical job it is, making a crown. He only uses the finest materials and best technicians. And a crown is vital, in my situation, or what's left of the tooth will fracture. No, a monster filling would not do.

I've now had the root-canal treatment. Compared with which, childbirth is a doddle. I know pain and agony and discomfort when I feel it and I'd rather have triplets. It's cost £350 so far and still doesn't feel right. I'm sitting here thinking: what should I do when it all settles down? Get myself crowned or what? It does seem sensible, I suppose, but it's not like a conservatory. It doesn't add value to my body should I want to sell it — and I've had the odd offer, you know. I can't invite people in, show them round the gold accessories and the amusing porcelain bonds.

And when I pack up this mortal coil, it will all have been a total waste. Nobody else will want my crown. One careful owner, hardly used.

 Bing Crosby was once asked on TV why he had such a relaxed manner. He put his hand in his pocket and pulled out a large wad of dollar bills. "That helps," he said.

PUTTING OFF THE POST

— £ —

I'm interested in money. But over there, in the corner, is a pile of money, or stuff containing or pertaining to my money, and for some reason I just can't get up the energy to look at it. What is happening to me?

We were away for four weeks in southern Africa, visiting our daughter in Botswana and also taking in Namibia. When we got back, there was the usual mass of post waiting to be dealt with. I did what I always do. Tore open anything that might contain cheques, then ran like hell to the bank. Next I dealt with the bills. I pay at once, always have done. My theory is that if you wait until the last moment, as most of the world does, especially when they are paying me, you don't really save much. We all go through life in a cycle of paying bills. Then you die. Whether you are always one month behind becomes meaningless. Each month you still have some bills to pay. And if you forget one, or it gets lost, you pay more.

I found I'd got behind with a Barclaycard Visa bill, with being away for four weeks. I rang to explain and guess what? The company cancelled the £20 interest charge. In the past, you see, I'd always paid on time. Moral: be good. You know it makes cents.

Then very slowly I plough through the unsolicited stuff, people wanting my old underpants for a charity auction, when of course I'm still wearing them. Or to speak at the Cockermouth Pea and Pie Annual Supper, no fee, but all the pies you can eat. You don't have to be at all well known these days to get such requests. I think half the world now spends its time asking the other half to do something. I call all these 'fan letters'. Not all are, in fact, many are downright abusive. "How could you have written such a thing, did you never learn to spell, why don't you check your facts, you ignorant northern, Spurs, capitalist idiot."

In the old days, you could spot abuse a mile off. The green ink and capital letters were a clue. Now in the high-tech age, you get halfway through a beautifully printed, 15-page letter before you realise, eh up, nutter alert. By that time you've lost half the morning.

The fourth pile concerns money. I always leave this to last. At this time of the year, it's enormous. So many investments I'd forgotten about have come up. There's a stupid capital accumulator plan I took out 10 years ago with Norwich Union and always regretted. It has now matured. In fact it's been lying, doing nothing, for eight weeks. Also, a two-year bond from Northern Rock and something from Scottish Widows. The money is there for me to collect or reinvest. I'm like a rabbit, caught in the glare of the financial world's headlights. They're all screaming at me buy, buy, and I can't decide.

There's also a mass of Pep annual statements, going back ages. I took them out, each year, being prudent, as Gordon Brown told us. Some have done well, I think. Others are rubbish, I'm sure. But because I don't want to be confronted by my own stupidity, I don't actually read any of them. Then, there's a mass of hurry, hurry, guaranteed monster interest rates, huge discounts if you invest now, don't be a loser, send off now.

Chase de Vere has somehow got hold of our London and Lakeland addresses and each post brings a sack load of special offers from the firm and other chancers, sorry financial advisers, whom I'm sure I have never contacted. I find myself picking up something that says Key Features, then drop it, arms and brain aching, when it turns out to be 50 pages in titchy type. I think the best thing to do with such excitements is leave them in a pile. When you eventually get round to reading them, with luck, you'll find the special offer expired on April 5. You can then bin them, having saved time and probably a fortune.

Isa, lovely girl, I know I really should do something about her. Now it's a new tax year, but this awful financial lethargy has overtaken me, as if of hemlock I have drunk. I've cut out about 20 Isa advertisements and coupons from the papers, all unread, now going yellow at the edges, but aren't we all? The trouble with the money world is that them out there, whose job it is, poor sods, are at it every day while we, even poorer sods, can only get our feeble minds round it now and again. We have other things to do, you see. Living, that's what it's called.

George Bernard Shaw was in negotiation to sell the film rights of one of his plays to Sam Goldwyn. There were long discussions which ended with Shaw deciding not to sell.

"The trouble is, Mr Goldwyn," said Shaw. "You are interested only in art while I am interested only in money."

PENSION PITTANCE

— £ —

I think I keep an eye on my money, so I tell myself. Always boring on about money, so my wife tells me. Very tight when it comes to money, so my children allege. Yet I keep surprising myself. If I'm so smart, how come I forgot all about my Sun Life of Canada personal pension plan?

Last week, the company wrote to tell me the plan has matured. Apparently, back in June 1980, I started a pension with the firm — £500 a year for 20 years. I remember the person who talked me into it, a canny Scot called Morag. Looking back, I can remember all the con-men — sorry, advisers — I allowed through the door with their dark suits, scrubbed faces, shiny briefcases. All very impressive till I found they'd come on the Underground and hadn't eaten for days.

There was that sweaty one who went on about his three failed marriages. The fat one who asked if he could have a bacon sandwich and sat stuffing his face instead of helping to stuff my bank balance. Where are they now? Retired or caught.

Of course I've been aware these past 20 years that £42 was going out of our account every month to Sun Life but I'd forgotten why. If asked by my dear wife, I'd have said: life insurance policy, don't you worry, pet. For all she knew, it could have been maintenance for a love child, gambling debts, sauna bills, or even worse, that dealer in football memorabilia I've been paying a fortune to.

So I rushed to find the original documents. I have in front of me what Morag estimated back in 1980. In June 2000, the fund value would be £39,000 from which I would get £12,000 tax free and a pension of £4,000 a year. I bet I was jolly pleased at the time, thinking of these riches.

I can remember what my salary was back in 1980, because I'd just left my job as editor of *The Sunday Times Magazine* on £10,000 a year. In 1980, I could have bought a flat for £12,000, while a £4,000 annuity would have paid for two months every year in Barbados. Today, you'd be lucky to get a tent for £12,000 while with £4,000 you might manage two weeks at Cobblers Cove, off-season. But I didn't know that, then. Or how puny my pension would turn out to be.

So what is it worth today? The fund total has proved pretty accurate: £36,000. It's the annuity which is so lousy. Sun Life of Canada is offering £1,752 a year, though it will go up 3% a year if I take that option, plus £7,000 in cash. I'm therefore going to get under half what I was promised—yet in real terms, taking into account inflation since 1980, it's about one twentieth of what I might have expected. Okay, don't tell me the inflation rates. I don't want to know. And yes, I have looked at the small print in 1980. It wasn't guaranteed. An interesting document, by the way — it contains handwriting and real typing, done by a real human being. Don't come across that today.

So what's the moral? The obvious one is that in 1980 I should have arranged a 20-year mortgage and bought a flat for £12,000. It would be worth £100,000 today, have given me 20 years of income, and now be all mine. Second, it makes me smile when all these teenage financial experts tell us how we must have pensions, churning out the same old stuff about the tax advantages and the wonderful annuities you will get. Ha ha, they wouldn't know a pension plan if they met it in their porridge. When you are 13, figures for 20 years ahead look brilliant. Not so brilliant when you get there and look backwards. Third, wipe it from your mind, and move on. I wonder if I could be a financial adviser when I grow up? No, too simplistic. You need graphs and charts and a shiny briefcase.

Because I'd forgotten this was a pension plan, thinking it was a life insurance thing, I haven't actually been worrying about possible annuities all these years. If I'd watched it carefully, I'd have been clutching my head at my stupidity. Now it's a nice little unexpected bonus. I think I will book Cobblers Cove for January. Might even buy a tent.

Nine million Britons suffer from a condition called Financial Phobia—and half the population shows symptoms. According to Egg, the world's largest on-line bank, sufferers are incapable of 'forming a consistent and productive relationship with their money.' The phobia includes behaviour such as not opening bank statements; never checking bank balances; throwing away or filing unopened statements. The very thought of trying to manage personal finances can lead to a racing heart (45%), feeling physically ill or dizzy (11%) or renders the sufferer immobilised (15%). Yet in other ways those afflicted by the condition are well-adjusted individuals. Financial phobes are found in all class and age groups—though the highest levels are among 16–24 year olds, and women in general are more likely to suffer. It may be triggered initially by a money problem such as a fall in the worth of life savings. It can also be caused by frustration at the time and effort needed to make sense of money issues, and the fear of not understanding pages of figures and small print.

Almost a quarter of sufferers would rather give up a day's holiday than balance their bank statement (the figure is 12% among non-sufferers) and nearly a third would rather go to the dentist.

FORGET DESIGNER GEAR — GIVE ME
CHEAP JUNK EVERY TIME

— £ —

When it comes to spending money, which I do all the time, there is one thing I'm really, really against: gear. By which I mean equipment, outfits, the stuff you are supposed to put on when you are about to take part in any activity. I admit people can look good and feel good when they dress up in the supposedly proper way, but when I see them coming, carrying all the clobber, my mind always thinks: you've been done, my old son, taken in, poor sap—you won't catch me with any of that stuff.

We used to go skiing when the children were young and of course they insisted on all the latest gear. I'd arrive on the slopes in my usual designer clothes—designed for my comfort, that is. Old cords, holey pullover and old sports jacket, all perfect for falling over in the snow. They'd refuse to speak to me. If it was really cold I might make an effort and put on a second pullover. Look around at what clothes you already have I'd tell them, and take them with you, but they wouldn't listen. And they had to have special ski socks greased from the oil of baby llamas. On safari, you always see the fattest, unhealthiest looking folks in all the latest co-ordinated designer khaki outfits. And they are convinced they look like that actress in *Something out of Africa* as opposed to Something out of Sid's Surplus Store in Kentish Town. (What's happening to it, by the way? I used to buy a lot of cheap gear there.)

On the beach, the gear is more minimal and these baggy shorts are certainly going to see me out. With sun specs, most people are posing, so I've never understood what's wrong with the cheapest pair from Boots. Boy soldiers in Africa, when posing with the latest guns, always have very cheap sunglasses. Doesn't seem to bother them.

My wife has always insisted you must buy the best sunglasses. She goes for the ones marked ultraviolet, UB40 or whatever, being very susceptible to advertising. She has gone through life saying you get what you pay for. So did I chortle when that report came out saying that a £3 pair can be just as effective as £300 specs.

For walking in Lakeland, I used to wear trainers in summer and wellies in winter and scoff at all those clumping about in hand-made boots at £120 a pair and anoraks made from dead penguins. Comfort is all, I say. Now I wear walking sandals, ones with Velcro straps. I think they are brilliant. The latest fetish in Lakeland is for trekking poles. They're sort of like ski poles, with a strap at the end. I have an advert for one in front of me that boasts three-section aluminium-alloy shafts, anodised inside and out, a carbide tip and a strong locking system. Dear God. Man managed with simpler equipment when he travelled to the moon. One small step, admittedly, but I don't remember any of them using a trekking pole. Yet people convince themselves these poles are necessary to get them out of the car in the Buttermere car park and into the Fish Inn. I even met a man strolling along Main Street, Cockermouth with his pole.

The theory is that they take the weight off your knees. Coming down a steep hill, I can see this might be useful, but not when walking round a lake on a flat path. But people love the image of themselves. By being equipped right, they think they are right.

I hate carrying anything when walking so I'd never dream of taking two extra bits of metal. And the price. You need two, which is £60 at least. I can cut two sticks for free from a hedge. The price, of course, is what's really behind all this blind prejudice. I am just too mean to spend such money, when I could buy, say, another black plastic clock. That's what I was doing in Cockermouth. They're only £1 each. Incredible. I rushed home and my wife said: "Put it straight in the garage, with the other clocks." But they're bargains, I say, absolute bargains. "We've got enough bargains," she said. "What you need is a decent pair of shorts. Not six stupid nasty clocks, just because they're cheap."

Slang terms for specific amounts of money:

Desmond	£4	Desmond Tutu (2 plus 2)
Taxi Driver	£5	
Pavarotti	£10	a tenor / tenner
Bobby Moore	£20	i.e. a score
Pony		£25
Hawaii	£50	from the TV series Hawaii 5-0
Monkey	£500	
Gorilla	£1,000	i.e. a large monkey
Archer	£2,000	The amount Lord Jeffrey Archer allegedly gave to Monica Coughlan as a bribe
Bernie	£1,000,000	the donation Bernie Ecclestone gave to the Labour election campaign

BEING A KEPT MAN IS NOT ALL IT'S CRACKED UP TO BE

— £ —

My wife earns more money than me. For four years now it's been happening and I don't mind admitting it. If I'd been my father, which I'm growing into every day (just look at the thinning hair, being unable to find things) I would probably have been ashamed, kept it quiet, pretended otherwise. But times change. There are loads of blokes out there in a similar position. Many of us are kept men.

I don't see it as a blow to my pride or position, even though we are in the same line of business, moving words around for a living. Her books have steadily earned more money over the years. Well done, pet. Mine have gone up and down.

I tell myself it's because I jump around, doing a different sort of book every time, the common denominator being my ignorance. She appeals to a similar sort of audience whether she does fact or fiction: women. Oh no, I didn't mean it. I mean intelligent readers, of all flavours.

I kept her for the first 30 years, so it's only fair she should take over the baton. But in one vital way she won't. She doesn't care about advances or sales, will accept what her publishers say. Even worse, she turns away money. There are novels she won't allow to be reprinted, ones she wrote years ago and now decides she never liked. "What are you doing?" I cry. "If some paperback firm wants to bring them out again, it's their affair, so let them."

I have always looked after all our so-called investments. Okay, mainly her investments now. When I say that, she says: "I don't want any investments, just leave it in the bank. Banks are safe, banks won't cheat you, will they?" Poor deluded person. She'll be telling me next that politicians are trustworthy and the tooth fairy is coming soon.

We've never had separate bank accounts or cheque books. One for all, I say, and I say it even louder now of course. So naturally our savings and stuff are jointly held. This means I often have to shove bits of paper under her pretty nose and say: "Sign here, my treasure." I don't do this when she's working. She would take no notice or tell me to go away. I don't want to interrupt her anyway, now she's our main breadwinner. In fact I'm often tempted to lock her door and tell her she's not coming out until she's written another best-seller. Okay then, I'll push some dry bread under the door if you get that chapter finished today.

But last week, after I had agonised for months over whether to put more money into our pensions and presented her with the forms, she suddenly said, "What's this for?" I started on the pros and cons, an argument that has gone round in my mind for years now, in which I've told myself: 'That's it, no more pension contributions, the returns are rubbish, bugger the so-called tax advantages', but then I always change my mind. God knows why, I must be potty. It's all right for you, I have to agonise these things out on my own.

"Spare me," she said. "Just where is it going? It could be going anywhere as far as I know."

"South America," I said. That's where it's all been going for the last four years. I've got four wives there, six mistresses, and when you wake up, I'll be orf.

"Look, it's going to the Equitable, we've used them for years, just sign on the dotted line and get back to your chapter. I want that book finished by October, or else."

I said it ever so nicely because I'd just thought of something. If and when no one wants my books and hers continue to do so well then I know what I'll do — I'll be her agent. We share everything, as I've said. But if I'm also getting 10%, I'll be doing better than her, won't I?

One in three British couples are financially incompatible according to research from Direct Debit.

- One in 10 women say their partner is financially disorganised and doesn't keep track of where money goes.
- 68% of women are responsible for looking after household bills.
- 75% of men completely trust their partner when it comes to money — 67% of women feel the same way.

The survey groups partners into four categories:

> Fiscal Friends,
> Cash Calamities,
> Dosh Delegators and
> Money Moaners.

FANTASY DISCOUNT THAT WENT
THROUGH THE ROOF

— £ —

So which should I choose? Last week I got carried away with two special offers, huge discounts, don't miss out, big summer sale, save 30%! That's what some double-glazing people promised. The other, from a firm I'd never heard of, which in my mind I keep calling Hotfeet, was also lavish with the adjectives and generous with the exclamation marks but its special summer discount is just 20%. None the less, I was salivating. Who wants to miss out on two summer bargains?

I don't know how their flyers got into our Lakeland house—perhaps secreted into a newspaper or brought by fairies in the night. We don't get leaflets stuck through the door round our way as we're miles from civilisation. One reason we leave London is that our NW5 hall becomes so jammed with mini-cab cards and takeaway Thai menus that if you don't get out around May, you're stuck inside, trapped until Christmas.

It so happened that the very day these leaflets materialised I had been up on a ladder to inspect a window frame that was rotting and also up in the loft to work out which slate was letting in rain. Hurrah, I thought. God, the paper boy or the fairies has sent solutions to my problems, just like that. I must have binned countless such leaflets over the years. I assume they keep pumping them out, at vast expense, because they know that by the law of averages, 1% of householders will suddenly respond.

I always used to tell my children when they were job hunting: don't give up, keep pumping out your CV, 'cos you never know, it might arrive on the desk of someone just at that very moment when they are looking to employ someone with his own collection of Judge Dredd magazines and a deep knowledge of all Spurs results from the 1988-89 season. That was about all my son could offer at the time but it worked. He got a job on the ice-cream counter at Marine Ices. He had to wear a white coat, which his dear mama washed and ironed for him, muttering the while to herself: "My son the doctor ..."

I rang the glazing firm and also Hotfeet and tried to get estimates. I wouldn't hold them to it, I said, just roughly what would two small double-glazed windows cost and how much might Hotfeet's special foam thingy roof system be? Neither would tell me. But I agreed to have their free estimate, still feeling excited by the huge summer discount. Spot the weakness in this excitement? Of course you can. If I didn't know the normal price, how would I know when it was discounted? They could quote me any old fantasy figure, then take away a fantasy discount.

They were both charming, the two salesmen who came, ever so clean, cheerful, even though one of them, from Hotfeet, had just suffered a bereavement in his family. And they had both driven miles, one had covered the length of the M6. I felt so guilty, bringing them all this way for small jobs I might never have done. Each complimented me on my lovely house and lovely garden, almost in the same words. I used to do this when I was interviewing people, thinking I was being ever so charming. I've vowed never to do it again. It comes out as pure smarm. Even though I do have a lovely house, etc.

The first estimate for the two windows, less their monster discount, is £767. I don't know whether that is good or bad, never having had any double glazing before. One doesn't, does one, or at least one keeps quiet about it. Hotfeet, with their fab discount, quoted £2,970 for my roof. Gulp. I'm sure it's a bargain and getting the roof done properly now will save thousands in the years to come, but it all began because I simply wanted a leak fixed. They couldn't just do that. I have to have the full treatment, which of course comes with excellent guarantees.

My wife said go on, take it, you mean thing, it'll be worth it. You brought that nice man all this way and he's just had a bereavement. She didn't care about the double glazing. The windows are hard to get to, so it will save getting up to paint them from now on. So I've said yes to the glazing firm. But I think I'll say no to Hotfeet. Seems a good company, very efficient, but I don't actually need them. I'm now left with a warm glow, having saved £2,970. Okay, a fantasy saving but it was the fantasy discounts that got me started.

Frugal Living UK is a website for those who want to reduce debts, find ways to save, live more simply, or just 'beat the system a little and end up with more cash.'

The website provides money saving tips in several areas. For example, cleaning:

1. Use a teaspoon of bicarbonate of soda on a damp cloth instead of expensive cleaners.

2. Use vinegar for cleaning surfaces such as glass.

3. Use essential oils for general cleaning — they're very economical as you use so little.

4. Use half the recommended amount of washing powder (unless your clothes are really filthy.)

5. If you need a special cleaning fluid for a particular job, try a 99p shop.

MONEY MATTERS

— £ —

Gather round, children, for a word in your ear. As you know, the government has decreed that from this month, personal finance will be taught in all of our schools from the age of five. Excellent news—money matters.

It matters more than ever because from now on we have to be responsible for ourselves, whether it is paying our mobile phone bill at primary school; for our gap year to 'find ourselves', our fines to be allowed out again having found ourselves; our fees through college; getting a mortgage; organising our own pension; popping back afterwards and paying our funeral director. It is up to us, folks. The government does not care any more.

What you do not know is that the government has asked me to be chief adviser on its national curriculum for teaching personal finance in schools. A very wise move, Mr Blair.

I should not really do this but here is a sneak preview of the

TEN BASIC RULES OF MONEY

to be taught in all schools, very soon.

1. You are here to be fleeced

No, I did not say conned and cheated, though that can happen. They do not actually want to take all your money away, not at once. They plan to come back and fleece you over and over again, all through life, forever. Just like sheep.

2. Do not trust any advert

As Stephen Leacock observed in 1924, advertising is the science of arresting human intelligence long enough to get money from it. With financial advertisements, they do not even bother to disguise what it is they are after.

3. Read the asterisks first

When it says in big capitals, GUARANTEED* or OUTSTANDING PERFORMANCE—17.7% PER YEAR** ignore the capitals and go straight to the very, very, very small print, sometimes almost invisible, in which you will find the rate is guaranteed for the next half hour and yes, it was 17.7% but only for 35 minutes, back in 1957.

4. Values can go up as well as down

Too true, squire. But what it actually means is their values go up while yours go down.

5. Phone free for leaflet and information

Free, only if you have about four years to hang on, waiting, listening to stupid music, complicated instructions, millions of options, then a disembodied voice either selling you deals you do not want or asking for passwords you never had.

6. Ignore all advice

I did not say do not ask for it. Do so by all means, get lots of it, study all the bumf, then ignore it. But do not throw it all away. They use high-class glossy paper, the big boys, excellent for making paper planes or cutting up for Christmas cards.

7. Always ask yourself what's in it for them

What is their deal, what is their commission, and if they are so clever, why aren't they on the beach in Barbados?

8. You are on your own

Not just in the great scheme of things, in life and the universe, but in money. You will be the loser, not them. You will be left alone, not them, the one wondering why you ever did it, the only one who will remember the stupid advice or trick advertisements you believed in at the time. Meanwhile, so you will be told, the adviser is no longer with us, gone to another branch, to Wormwood Scrubs, that department has closed, we now operate under a different name, our new owners are in the Turks and Caicos Islands, you forgot to read the small print, any more of this and you will be hearing from our lawyers.

9. In the end you won't win

People with rose-coloured wall charts remember when interest rates were oh, up to 13%, really good, those were the days, eh, back in the 1960s, wish we had them now. They forget that inflation was also enormously high. Result—you hardly gained anything. Looking ahead they will tell you about the good times to come, how saving twopence a week now, when you are aged five and half, means you will be worth £10m at 55. Do not believe it. In fact do not believe anything about past rates. They are all fiddles, arranged to suit themselves. Or future rates and returns—they are fantasies. Someone will rearrange the furniture, so you will not beat them. The best to hope for in life is that you will not lose.

10. Hunt's Last Rule

You can never be too rich or have too many corkscrews. Thank you. Now eat these rules after reading them or you will be accused of cheating in the end-of-term exams.

Energy saving tips:
1. Switch off appliances at the wall before going to bed at night. Many electrical items use electricity even while off if connected to an outlet.
2. Switch off the oven, hotplate and iron a few minutes before you need to stop using them—they will stay hot for a long time. Heating devices use more power than anything else.
3. Switch a kettle off by hand—the automatic cut off will leave it boiling and burning up watts for longer.
4. Invest in a solar powered battery charger for long term savings.
5. Tumble drying is very expensive—line drying is free.
6. If your heating is on a timer or thermostatic control, try switching it on and off by hand as needed, this uses less fuel.
7. Put special insulation sheets behind radiators to reflect the heat back into them or use cardboard wrapped in aluminium foil.

NUMBERPLATE FOR SALE:
ONE CARELESS OWNER

— £ —

I've done something really out of character. How can I face my family? How will I hold up my head in decent Hampstead intellectual company? What will my accountant say?

I got this letter out of the blue, at my home address, from a firm called Alpha One offering me a chance to buy the car numberplate M2 EHD. 'Such exclusive registrations tend to be snapped up quickly,' it trilled. 'Don't delay. Take this remarkable opportunity and in just a few weeks, your car will be displaying that ultimate individual touch.' I was about to bin it when I thought: that's funny, how do they know my full initials are EHD? I have gone through life disguising the fact. Not deliberately. Just convenience. I was christened Edward Hunter Davies but from birth I have never been called Edward, always Hunter. Now and again at school a visiting nurse, doing a nit inspection, would study her notes and say: "Edward, come here" and I would look around, wondering who it was.

I once revealed the truth to Paul McCartney when he was on holiday with us in Portugal. He immediately got his guitar and sang me a song. "There you go Eddie, Eddie; there you go Eddie, Eddie you've gone." That's all I can remember. Don't think he ever recorded it. Paul is of course not his first name. He was actually christened James Paul. Could he have tipped off Alpha? No, he's got better things to do. Who's Who, that must be where they got it from. I do admit the Edward bit, in brackets. Out of curiosity, I rang Alpha. They denied they'd used Who's Who. Their basic lists come from the electoral roll which they buy from a company then put on their computers, according to initials. I said there must be hundreds if not thousands in Britain with the initials EHD. They surely can't contact them all? No, because they also cross check with postcodes. Posh I certainly am, yet 35 years ago, when we moved into our north London house, we were going downmarket, slumming it on the wrong side of the heath. Now our address has zoomed up, zoned up. Thanks of course to me living here. By using the electoral roll, they had also discovered my wife's christian name, Margaret. Hence they were offering M2 EHD.

Pretty smart, though they were not to know that in fact my wife never drives, has no interest in cars, hates cars. I'm not interested in cars either, certainly not their registrations. I don't even know my own and I've had it three years. But in talking to the Alpha man, I became fascinated by the whole world of what's called 'cherished numbers'. Yes, I've seen them advertised in the newspapers, acres of them, but never read them. Have you seen the size of the type? Apparently the most expensive number sold at auction was K1NGS which made £250,000. Unbelievable. Anything that makes a word can go for a small fortune. If it's just initials like the one they were offering me, then £360–£500 is the norm. Mine at £360 was obviously a cheapo, bottom-of-the-range model.

"As a bit of fun," I said to my wife. "Could you pretend that you and the children have bought it for me for Christmas? Don't let on I bought it for myself."

"Certainly not," she said. "If you buy something so silly I won't speak to you again."

I happened to be on the phone to my brother-in-law and I remembered he'd bought a cherished number, 1CPF, for his son Christopher Paul Forster on his 21st. He paid £1,400 for it back in 1980. Strewth, that was a lot.

"Yes," he said. "But today it's worth around £10,000." How does he know? Because he reads every line of every advert in every paper. But then he does have excellent eyesight. So it's not silliness or vanity having one's own individual number. It's an investment, innit? Secondly, it will be jolly handy, always having the same number-plate, regardless of the car. I'm bound to remember it, eventually. So I bought it. I've just received the certificate of entitlement for the vehicle registration mark M2 EHD from the DVLA people in Swansea. Looks great. No, not got it on my car yet.

It's my own fault, really. I wasn't quite concentrating. My present car is a K registration model, which I'd forgotten. The number I've bought is an M. It's illegal to put an M plate on a K car. So I'll have to wait till I buy an M plate or a later car, which might not be for years. In the meantime, does anyone want to buy M2 EHD? I've cherished it for more than a week. Surely it must be worth 10 grand by now.

British places with money names:

Penny Bridge – Cumbria
Pennyfuir, Pennyghael, Pennygown – Argyll and Bute
Pennyglen – South Ayrshire
Pennymoor – Devon
Shillingford – Devon, Oxfordshire
Shillingstone – Dorset
Shillington – Bedfordshire
Pound Bank – Worcestershire
Pound Green, Poundgate – East Sussex
Pound Hill – West Sussex
Poundffald – Swansea
Poundisford – Somerset
Poundland – South Ayrshire
Poundon – Buckinghamshire
Poundsbridge – Kent
Poundsgate – Devon
Poundstock – Cornwall
Dollar, Dollarbeg – Clackmannanshire
Dollar Law – Scottish Borders

PRICES MATTER BUT VALUES ARE
WHAT REALLY COUNT

— £ —

I've just been out to buy a packet of Pampers disposable nappies, £5.99 for 34, plus some Johnson's baby wipes at £2.50 for 80. What am I doing? Sitting here saying: I can't believe it. I can't believe the prices and I can't believe such stuff exists and that people are actually buying it.

When we had our last baby, 28 years ago, it was towelling nappies. You used them until they were threadbare or the baby started secondary school, whichever came first. As for baby wipes, they didn't exist. Now you mention it, babies in the Sixties and Seventies must have had pretty yucky bums. I was also told to buy some jars of baby food, organic only. The word organic put me right off. I see the word organic and I reach for my gurn (Cumbrian word for a stupid face). Organic has only one meaning to me — expensive. The price in our local shop for something called SMA was 90p for a titchy sachet. We fed a family of five on that for a week in ye olden days. So I came home and lied, said they were fresh out.

Our daughter Caitlin and baby Ruby are visiting, so joy all round but also baby gear all round. We've had to tool up, buy or borrow, and now have a pram and pushchair in the hall again, toys all over the place, a state-of-the-art baby alarm crackling away, a baby seat in the car, a cot in the bedroom and a highchair in the kitchen. How do modern parents manage? I read somewhere, or made it up, that it now costs £1m to feed, clothe and educate each child in the Western world until they're 21. And £2m if it's on organic food.

My first reaction, when buying all this stuff, was to cluck away about the prices without really thinking. Until we got to Ikea and bought the highchair. It was only £12. What a bargain. Let's buy two, I said. One for when Ruby's dirtied the first one. I'm surprised there aren't disposable highchairs. I've a feeling Caitlin's highchair cost about £12 in the Sixties. In fact, if I do some sums, allowing for inflation, remembering the cost of a Bovril when I was a lad, I wonder if things on the whole have got more expensive?

We all do this, we over-50s, immediately exclaiming at modern prices. Then we bore everyone by remembering when beer was only twopence a pint, the best seat at Spurs was a shilling and a flat in Hampstead was six guineas a week. Having bored them, we send them straight to sleep by saying hold on, what's that in modern money?

One rule of thumb says multiply by 20 to understand Sixties prices today. So let's see. My first Mini, which I bought in 1963, cost £500. Multiply by 20 and that's

£10,000 — about right for a basic car today. I was earning £20 a week in 1960. Today, I suppose it must be 30 times as much. We bought our London house in 1964 for £5,000. It's worth at least £500,000 today. That's 100 times as much. On the other hand, when we flew to Ibiza for our hols in 1962 the flight cost £50. In theory, that's £1,000 in today's money — and yet it's not. You can get cheap flights to Ibiza for only £100. Many domestic items, such as fridges and televisions, have grown much cheaper over the decades. As have most foods.

I do have the bills for the initial work we had done on this house, when we bought it, and they're roughly in line with inflation. London plasterers and plumbers were on 15 shillings an hour in 1964. Now it's 20 to 30 times as much. If you can get them.

My wife always wishes she'd kept swatches of all the curtains and carpets, little samples of wallpaper, slices of tiles, that we've had in this house over 36 years, just to remind her of patterns gone by. It's bills gone by I love but I can't find their babyhood bills for prams and cots. Perhaps it's just as well. I must stop going on about old prices. Madness lies that way. You can't compare. Live for today.

Don't count the cost. But always remember: as life goes on, money is meaning less.

Jean Agassiz, the Swiss naturalist who in 1848 became Professor of Zoology at Harvard, was asked by a learned society to address its members. Agassiz declined, saying he had too much research work to do. The man persisted, indicating that there would be a handsome payment, if he agreed to the talk.

"That's no inducement to me," replied Agassiz. "I can't afford to waste my time making money."

THE TAX MAN COMETH

— £ —

I've just had a letter from the taxman. How kind of him to write out of the blue when I don't owe him any money — just a short, crisp letter. I opened it and groaned. "Oh no, oh God! We are about to be investigated," I shouted to my dear wife over the muesli.

"It's actually for you, pet," I said. "It says the taxman is going to make some inquiries into your returns and has written to our accountant for certain information."

I then rang our accountant and screamed at him. "I bet it's your fault," I shouted. "You've told him to do this just because I wouldn't join your stupid insurance scheme." Some months ago the accountant sent me details of an insurance scheme his firm was introducing. Apparently the Revenue is now doing random investigations. You can have done nothing wrong at all but it'll pick on certain people and go through their books, demanding proof of every postage stamp they've ever bought. It can go on for months and months, driving you round the bend.

It can also prove very costly, even if it turns out okay. Accountants, like lawyers, always do jolly well when terrible things happen to their clients. But for the small sum of £160 each per year, I was offered an insurance policy that would cover us for up to £5,000 extra accountancy costs. "Get lost," I said. "I'm not paying that."

I have an aversion to all forms of insurance. Some of course you can't avoid, but I've never knowingly taken out a life insurance policy or any sort of health insurance. I refuse even to join the AA or RAC. I was in the AA for a year about 30 years ago. That was when they wore leather chaps and saluted you. So it was well worth it. My Mini Traveller broke down one day. We were on the way up to Carlisle, full of screaming kids, and an AA man whizzed past on the other side—and didn't stop. Perhaps he didn't see me, but that was the end of that. I cancelled my subscription and for the next 30 years did without.

Fortunately, I haven't broken down since but even when I do, I'll be quids in. The money saved in subs will easily cover any breakdown costs I might have. "It's up to you," said my accountant. "But we are advising our clients that it's sensible to insure." We have nothing to hide, I said. Our books are straightforward. Surely it's impossible for you to run up a bill for £5,000 on our behalf. He just smiled — on the phone of course. But I can always detect an accountant's smile.

So it was most spooky, the way I'd refused to insure one day and the next day the call came. Perhaps it was Atlas, god of insurance, who used to carry the globe on his head for the Prudential (or am I getting mixed up?) and not my accountant who said: "Let's get Hunt. Thinks he's smart, huh? We'll show him."

I went out into the garage, which led to more effing and blinding. You have to keep all your records for seven years, so I've been told. I'd put the ones now six or seven years old into plastic bags and stashed them in the garage but it's been letting in water for months now, with all the rain. And one plastic bag for 1993 was well and truly sodden. Oh no.

What if their inquiry refers to a haircut bill for a Border Television interview in 1993? And I find the rain has ruined it, will she go to prison? I fretted for two weeks, all on my own. I tried to explain it to my wife but got nowhere. I'm the self-appointed money man, or at least the only one interested.

Then last week the Revenue finally told us what the inquiry was. It was one very simple request — to see proof of my wife's pension contribution to Equitable Life for last year. My accountant already had it in his office. So he sent it straight off to them. If he charges me more than one first class stamp extra for his efforts, then I really will moan.

 Self-employed handyman Joe Temeczko was known in his Minneapolis neighbourhood for being a skinflint. The Polish immigrant had no family and worked as a handyman, carpenter and roofer.

In order to save money he got free food from local charities, bought day-old bread and read newspapers in the shop rather than buying them. He also filled his modest home with things he salvaged from the street, which he then tried to sell. A neighbour, Rod Carlson, told a local paper that Temeczko sometimes tried to flog things that Carlson himself had thrown out. "He would come up to you and say, 'How about $12 for this box?' I'd say, 'Joe, these things are mine.' He'd take them and say, 'How about $9?'"

But far from being impoverished, Temeczko had managed to amass an estate of around $1 million. Shortly after the 9/11 attacks, he re-wrote his will and left $1.4 million to the City of New York. He died a few weeks later at the age of 86. The money has been used for park renovation and The Daffodil Project, a memorial to the 9/11 victims.

CHAPTER THREE

Old shoes, a new Jag, premium bonds, and best of all, a free bus pass

— £ —

INEQUITABLE EQUITABLE

One of the problems of having money and possessions is losing them. It must have been so simple living in a cave, not having to worry about tax bills, pensions, credit cards, shares, investments and what the hell Equitable Life might be doing. Not that I'm talking about Equitable. I'm trying to blank the firm, pretend it never existed, that we never met.

Okay then, just three paragraphs. I gave Equitable almost all my worldly savings — in the form of my lifetime's pension fund. Three years ago, I cashed it in to buy an annuity, the theory being that as the rates were so low I might as well start drawing out now, before they got worse. This proved correct. But guess what I did with the money? We are still earners, me and my dear wife, paying higher tax, so I decided not to spend it but plough all our pension income back into something called a 10-year maximum investment plan, with, wait for it: Equitable.

It means I am lumbered with two appalling deals, each dropping in value all the time. And I can't get out of them. I must have been off my trolley. Hence I'm not talking about the Equitable. I was cursing the company and my own stupidity when my wife announced that her purse had gone, probably stolen. It contained her Gold Visa card, Switch card and Marks & Spencer charge card. You hear all these tales of huge bills run up in minutes on a stolen credit card by some kid. With three cards, there's probably a gang already in Barbados, in their Marks & Spencer casuals, on their 20th rum punch of the day at Cobblers Cove, which is where we happen to be going next week. How the hell am I going to get the cards cancelled and new ones issued before we go away? I do have some sort of insurance, where you ring one number and they cancel them all for you, which I did. But with going away so soon, I didn't want to take any chances, so I rang the three credit-card people direct, which of course took forever. They asked for the password, security number, mum's maiden name, dad's favourite football team, any embarrassing moments, the number you first thought of. It only took all day. So that was quick.

The insurance people said we would be covered for any loss, but we needed to report it to the police and get a reference number. I went to the cop shop in Hampstead where, of course, there was a long queue. A posh woman, the wife of a lord, so it transpired, was reporting the loss of her husband's car and even worse, so she said, the thieves had got his House of Lords parking permit. Some people will stop at nothing. Then a lunatic with staring eyes and a bulging briefcase burst in, swore and shouted at the copper behind the counter. Several people left the queue, worried what he might produce from his briefcase. The copper was on his own, so every time he had to go elsewhere in the building to check something he had to bring down an iron grille and close his counter, just in case anyone nicked anything.

After nearly two hours waiting, I was practically screaming. I decided the briefcase man was not a lunatic but an ordinary member of the community just trying to get served, or an Equitable Life pensioner, desperate for someone to shout at. When it was my turn, I was asked where my wife last saw her purse. "In Marks & Spencer," I said.

"Ah," said the copper. "Private property. We don't deal with that." "Okay then," I said. "In the street." Eventually he allowed me to fill in a property lost in street form. I got a copy for the insurance company. All of this fiddling around took up about two days of what's left of my life. And turned out to be totally pointless.

This morning my wife got a letter from London Transport's lost property department. Her purse had been found on a bus. It hadn't been stolen after all. And everything is intact. Ah well, it did fill up my mind for two days, stopped me raging against the inequities of a certain assurance society, the one I'm not talking about. They know who they are.

An internet poll conducted by CNN asked what people would rather spend $1 million on—
themselves or their heirs?

Total response: 32,189

Spend $1 million on yourself?   70%

Spend $1 million on your heirs?   30%

LAPPING UP BARGAINS

— £ —

I seem to have spent half my life wandering up and down Tottenham Court Road, comparing the prices of things I do not really want but have convinced myself I should really have.

Tottenham Court Road in London is devoted to shops selling electrical stuff—from computers and hi-fi to video cameras. It's a good place to buy as there is a huge selection in a small area. You can walk up and down for 100 yards, on either side of the road, compare prices on similar or identical items, visit about 30 shops—and end up a total wreck. So many times have I come home no wiser, my mind completely befuddled, buying nothing. Last week, I spent three hours and I bought something. Now I'm ready for intensive care.

They always have the latest models, the newest gizmos you have never seen before and can't believe will ever catch on. I go to Tottenham Court Road when I feel an urge to catch up with civilisation. I bought our first video there, having said videos were a nonsense. I never watch television enough to justify a video, so why do I want one? I said the same about fax machines; now I can't live without it. I've bought three photocopiers over the years, all excellent bargains.

My earliest purchase was a silent film camera on which I captured all the children. Then I moved on to smaller and smaller camcorders. My present one is not digital, as I am usually one stage behind the latest. My theory is that you can negotiate the best prices if you're not after the newest model.

In those three hours, I kept on bumping into the same people doing the same thing, trudging up and down, getting rattier and rattier, lying and saying that two doors down that model was cheaper. I did this as well, even though I know that they know next door's prices. All the same, in each shop, they have their targets, stuff they are trying to shift quickly, so you can always negotiate. Guess what I was after? Something I said I would never buy. For more than 10 years now I have worked on an Amstrad word processor, a PCW9512. In fact, I have two, one in London, one in Lakeland. Each cost £300. I love them. I must have shifted about two million words on them in the past 10 years. Mostly the same words. I do have a limited vocabulary. They do exactly what I want and have never let me down.

I get ridiculed all the time by writing chums who boast about the wonderful things their state-of-the-art computers can do, the marvels of email, the bliss of the internet, neither of which I can get on my prehistoric Amstrad.

I decided against a normal computer. They are so ugly, all those nasty white bits, towers and pylons, taking up so much space. So I went looking for a laptop. One reason for looking now is that it's a seasonal ritual, trailing up and down Tottenham Court Road at the end of January to see how cheap I can get something. The other reason is that Caitlin, our older daughter, is still with us from Botswana. She is a computer whizz who is going to get it working.

I bought something called a Compaq Notebook 100 for £763, including bits and bobs, having got them down by about £100, good, eh? If you know where I could have got it cheaper, don't tell me. I won't use it. Not personally. All I have done is acquire it. I now have it in the house. It's visible proof that I am alive and kicking and up to date.

 "All things are obedient to money."

The first recorded written version of this proverb was around BC 68 when the Roman poet Horace came out with it in his Satires. Geoffrey Chaucer in 1390 in the *Canterbury Tales* repeated the observation, almost precisely in the words we use today. "Alle thynges obeyer to monye."

YOUTH OF TODAY ARE GETTING
RICH QUICKER

— £ —

I was talking to a friend the other day and he came out with a phrase I've been thinking about ever since— that's when I haven't been thinking about whether Carlisle United will avoid relegation and why southern people pronounce Eddie Stobart as Stow-bart not Stobburt, as it should be. "Affluence is getting younger." That was the phrase. It was used by Richard Williams, chief executive of Sandy Lane, the poshest, most expensive hotel in the Caribbean.

Richard was going on about the world's wealthy getting younger and I didn't quite believe him. "You have to be incredibly well off to afford Sandy Lane," I said. "So surely most of your customers are getting on a bit." ""Not at all," he said. "In 1992 the average age of the clientele was 55. When Sandy Lane closed in 1997 the average had dropped to 47. So next month, when it opens again, it will be aiming at an even younger age group. Hence the slightly more relaxed attitude to dress. Jeans will now be allowed at dinner."

"Disgusting," I replied. "What has happened to standards?"

It's a generalisation that affluence is getting younger but is there any truth in it? Ten years ago, from where I was sitting, looking around at the world, I would definitely have said the opposite. When our three dear children were still at home, hanging around the house, looking as if they would be students for ever, I used to think that when they do leave home, we'll never see them again. They won't be able to afford to live in this area.

House prices had shot up, so how could any young couple with children ever afford our streets ever again, the way we had done. I was 26 when we moved here, a young journalist, and my wife, a teacher, was 24. Our neighbours were similar. Today, nobody from those professions, or at that age, could even afford a room in our street.

So 10 years ago I was thinking that our street would become a ghetto for oldies: no prams in the street, no climbing frames in the garden, no babies crying in the night. Yet now, when houses in our area will soon be hitting the £1m mark, we already have quite a few new young families with young children. They are in their late thirties rather than their twenties, but still of an age I never thought we'd see again as neighbours. Where have they got all the money from?

In the 1960s in London, there were young people with big money, such as pop stars and photographers. I remember David Bailey astonishing his neighbours in

Primrose Hill by buying a big house and painting the windows black. But young affluence was limited mainly to fashion or music. Footballers were paupers at the time. Now a whole range of young people are big earners, buying big houses in expensive areas and they're mostly the professional or management classes. We all know about the City whizz-kids and IT millionaires but behind them are some equally young lawyers and accountants, doing jolly well and working awfully hard. At one time, in such professions, you had to put in the years and work through the hierarchy. Now everything is speeded up. Life, communications, the whole shooting match — including making money. Millions are made in a moment, careers are created on one deal, firms go public in their lunch hour. And of course they can fall just as quickly. Not that they seem to care much. Lash out on the big house now, before it all crumbles.

We are talking about a tiny proportion of the population but it's not just in London. Manchester, Birmingham and Edinburgh have all got big suits in their thirties earning huge salaries. And while this small group coins it in, the gap between them and the rest of the population grows bigger. Young teachers and nurses, who have also put in many years in education and training, are left behind, unable to afford any house in London.

The way things are going I probably will end up living in a ghetto — but of young people not old people.

And I don't think I'll take a holiday at Sandy Lane, even if I could afford it.

UK's richest people aged 30 and under
(*The Sunday Times*, 2004):

1. Jonathan Rowland, 28   660 million
   Finance

2. Nina Hagen, 22   225 million
   Finance

3. Karl-Johan Persson, 29   181 million
   Inheritance

4. Mark Shuttleworth, 30   170 million
   Internet services

5. The Earl of Pembroke, 25   152 million
   Land, art

BURIED TREASURE WAS BARELY
WORTH FINDING

— £ —

I have just turned 65. To celebrate, I was having a clear out, going through some old papers. In one, dated 1970, the following sentence jumped out: 'A pension of £253 and three shillings per annum will be preserved for you, payable when you reach the age of 65.'

I bet at the time it sounded quite good. I might even have thought: "Oh goodie - if and when I ever reach that age, I'll be rolling in it, lucky old me." That is doubtless why I put it carefully in a drawer and forgot about it. Now, I cannot even remember what shillings were. As for £253 a year, that's hardly worth getting out of bed for today, especially as I find getting out of bed hellish at my age. Then I thought: "I'm not letting these beggars get away with it, whoever they are. Why should they hang on to my money, however piddling it might be?"

On the other hand, it might not be piddling. You see these weaselly worded adverts, which I always scoff at, where they claim that if you'd put £10 into some fund 25 years ago, it would be worth £1m today. It's always a fund you've never heard of, which probably never existed, except in their imagination. But perhaps mine is the example that will prove their claim, justify their boast? After all, over 30 years it's bound to have increased a lot, if just by inflation.

I studied the document carefully. It was from De Falbe Halsey (Life and Pensions) of 18 Finsbury Circus, London. It took me only a day to discover they had gone, rolled over, passed away. In 1970, they were handling insurance for *The Sunday Times*, where I had been on the staff from 1960–70, and had paid into the firm's pension fund.

I rang *The Sunday Times*. Its pension department said that my pension had been inherited by Thomson Newspapers, a completely different organisation. Oh no. Is it worth it? I find I'm always asking myself that question in relation to money. I look at all my rubbish Peps and my Isa, thinking what a waste of time. And as for my Equitable Life investments, did I mention I'm not mentioning them? Should I get shot of them? Can I really be bothered faffing around, making phone calls, reading small print, paying more charges and hidden fees, just to get my precious savings away from one load of chancers — sorry, long-established financial firms — and into another. In the end I'll probably be earning only 0.5% more, if that. Doing nothing, that is always so much less tiring. But what if I was now sitting on a small fortune? Why let Thomson have it any longer?

I eventually tracked down its address, found the appropriate department and a very helpful man looked up his records and told me that, yeah, I was on his list, the owner of an unclaimed pension. So why hadn't Thomson contacted me? He said the company did not have my address. "Oh, come on," I said. "I have been in the same house since 1964."

"Ah," he said, "When Thomson inherited the documents, it did not inherit addresses." In fact, it had recently asked the DSS to track down missing people. The DSS found some but is still holding unclaimed pensions for 70 people. There is a total of more than £100m out there, unclaimed, being kept by organisations to whom it does not belong. Camelot has about £30m in unclaimed winnings. National Savings and Premium Bonds are much the same. Then there are share certificates in lofts, bonds in bottom drawers, investments still held by dead investors. I made up that £100m figure. But I bet it's about right. Look, I haven't got time to do proper research. I've got my pension to track down.

And I got it in the end. Guess how much it's worth today? Thirty years of lying there, growing away, accumulating accumulations. Oh go on, guess. Make an old man amused. The answer is £275.89 per annum, though there is also a tax-free lump sum of £827, which is nice. I'm in the money, folks. All the same, I cannot help wondering what my pension fund has been doing. It's almost exactly the annuity they promised me 30 years ago. Surely someone, some firm, somewhere, must have gained by having it, taken advantage of it, not just left it lying around, doing nothing. Ah, money, it's all so mysterious.

Celebrities careful with money, allegedly:

Rod Stewart
When Rod was wrongly charged for a £4 bottle of mineral water at a restaurant in LA, he made a 20 mile round trip to get the amount re-credited to his credit card.

David Schwimmer
Schwimmer, who plays Ross on *Friends*, vowed never to visit a certain Hollywood liquor store again after a manager refused to give him a discount on six bottles of champagne.

Donald Dewar
Scotland's late First Minister heated his Glasgow living room with a two-bar electric fire and boiled a kettle for shaving.

BUYING SHOES TAKES A LOT
OF SOUL SEARCHING

— £ —

I was in the changing room at London's Kentish Town baths, getting undressed for my midweek swim, when I sensed a naked bloke watching me. I shoved my stuff in a locker, then turned round quickly to find him staring into my shoes. "Just admiring them," he said, apologetically. "I quite fancy a pair like that. How much were they?"

They are called Wolverine and the assistant said they were guaranteed for six months. I'd left the shop before I asked what that meant. Guaranteed to be shoes, presumably, so if they turn into a fridge or a bag of potatoes, they will replace them. The point about the shoes was that a) they had cost me a fortune and b) my wife had rubbished them, saying they looked horrible, were too big and a nasty colour. So when I got home, did I boast about this man with obviously excellent taste who had just admired my purchase.

They cost, I can hardly dare repeat it, £65. Gulp. This may not seem a lot to you, or a teenager, but it was a world record for me. I have gone through life spending no more than £20 on a pair of shoes. For £65, I told my wife, I could have bought a car. I don't know what came over me. A moment of wild extravagance, so out of character.

I can spend £500 on an 1896 book about footballers for my collection, which I did last week, or £2,000 on club class flights to Barbados as in January, or give my children £3,000 each for a Tessa, which I did when they first came out. Nobody can say I'm a meanie, but I find spending money on boring things such as clothes awfully hard.

With clothes, I always say: "Clothes? I've got clothes, why do I need any more clothes?" From my long experience, cheap clothes last just as long as expensive clothes. And you don't have to worry about them or get them dry-cleaned. The resale value of all clothes, regardless of cost, is negligible. So what's the point? I also have a more up-to-date and modern rationale for not spending money on clothes. I might get mugged if I walk around like a toff.

When I read about these flash gits with £4,000 Rolexes on their wrists, I think they are asking for it. How can they spend such money? My £4 watch, which I don't actually wear, but keep on the hall shelf and sometimes take with me if I'm planning to get somewhere roughly on time, tells just the same time as a £4,000 watch.

Keeping the house from falling down, I can just about spend money on that, if I grit my teeth. When it's something new, an addition or definite improvement, I can tell myself that it's an investment, putting up the value. The painters are doing the outside of our house at the moment, first time for five years. I don't know why we bother. In another five years, it will have to be done again. This time it's costing £2,400. I could have bought a house for that not long ago. New furniture, I also find that tough. Behind my back, my wife has given away a couch I have lolled on each evening for 35 years with my quiet drink and noisy evening paper. It will see me out, I've been saying for the past 10 years, every time she threatened to get a new one. She has now ordered one from the Sofa Workshop at vast expense which will come in six weeks. I said: "Six weeks? I could make one in that time." What's wrong with the second-hand furniture shop near the Tube? They have got loads on the front pavement, ready to be taken away, no need to wait.

When I say 'vast expense' I have no idea about the width or depth or breadth of the cost of this new sofa she has ordered. Let it be her little secret. I am starting a new system. When it comes to spending money on stuff I hate spending money on, she will sign all the cheques, then eat the bills. So I will never know the cost.

I have asked my wife to buy my shoes and clothes from now on and not tell me how much they cost. I splashed out on those shoes, yet she hates them, so it will benefit her. She refuses, the rotten thing. If you ask me, she's the mean one.

"Money is round and rolls away."
1619 proverb, found in a book called *Help to Discourse*. Still as neat and true as ever. Should be with us for a while yet, till credit cards take over the world.

"Money is wise, it knows its way."

Typical of all proverbs, really, you can just as easily find one that says roughly the opposite of what someone has just sagely observed. This was being said by clever sods around the same time as the above proverb, for it was collected in a book of proverbs by J. Ray in 1678.

IMPULSIVE CAR DEAL PAYS OFF IN THE END

— £ —

I saw a car advertised in the local paper, so I rang up and asked if they'd take my old one in part exchange. They said yes, maybe. I then asked if they could bring the car to my house, now, to let me see it, as we were going away. I expected them to say no chance, which I would have seen as a sign — a sign from the heavens meaning don't buy a new car. But the car came, brought by Paul, the salesman, an ex-policeman, ex-professional boxer, so he told me. Car salesmen never lie, so it must be true. In 40 minutes I had bought it.

My wife, who believes I have been utterly stupid, is not talking to me. I still can't believe it myself—I'm usually so careful with money. Yet I've now gone and done all the things I said I'd never do. First, I bought the car from a dealer. I made a vow years ago never to buy from a dealer because you are bound to pay about 20% more. I bought my last car privately four years ago from a stranger. He wanted £11,000 for a K-reg Jaguar that had done 67,000 miles. I got him down to £10,000 and felt pretty pleased. I was taking a chance but it paid off. No problems with it at all. It was my first Jag. I just woke up one day thinking: I'd like to have a Jag in this life. Why should John Prescott have all the fun? So I bought one—in British racing green, a very discreet colour that won my wife's approval. I've loved driving it. In fact it's never felt like driving, more like gliding. Second, I never even haggled, which is not like me. That's part of the fun, arguing the toss over pennies. In the advert, it said £12,995. It seemed reasonable for a P-reg Jag with 50,000 miles on the clock. I said I wanted £3,000 for my old one. He agreed. He took mine and I paid him £10,000—if only all transactions were so quick and easy.

The reasons why my dear wife thinks it's so mad are numerous. First, we were leaving two days later to drive 300 miles, with all our stuff, to Lakeland. My old car was perfect, I'd always said that. What if this new, unknown car broke down on the M6 outside Birmingham?

There was simply no need to get another one, certainly not at this time. Daft, she called it. Second, the colour. I'm colour blind. I have trouble telling grey from blue from green and don't care either way. It said in the paper the car was blue. But when it arrived even I could see it was turquoise — a sort of shrieking metallic turquoise — and what it was shrieking was 'flash git in a Jag'. I smiled at the colour.

She refused even to go out and look at it. I've forgotten to mention something, a little element in all this that has created more derision in my family than anything I've done for years. Even counting the days when I had bushy sideburns. And those white flares. Forgotten them. And the pink button-up grandpa vest. I should have destroyed that photo. Last year when I bought a personalised number plate, M2 EHD, I hadn't realised I couldn't put it on my K-reg Jag. It can't go on a car older than the numberplate. So for about a year I've been vaguely looking out for an M-reg or later Jag, but had given up until I suddenly saw that ad. My official rationale for swapping cars has been that because my old Jag's done 86,000 miles, it's about time I traded it in for a newer model with fewer miles. Before things go wrong, dear. It's only sensible, pet.

But of course I haven't been sensible. I have been wilful. And created a lot of faffing around for myself with the DVLA paperwork. You wouldn't believe the complications of buying a car with one number plate and changing it to another. Not to mention having to change the tax disc and the insurance certificate. Sometimes I wish I had no money. Then I wouldn't be able to spend any and get into these messes — not being spoken to, ringing all these people, giving myself a headache from worrying.

Of course I worried. All the way to Lakeland, I knew that if we broke down it would be completely my fault. But we didn't. And now we are here, safely. The flash git has landed. As I write, sheep in the adjoining field, who have had more than enough to put up with in recent months thanks to foot and mouth, are being dazzled by a turquoise glow.

George Raft, the film actor, earned and spent some ten million dollars in his working life. "Part of it went on gambling," so he later explained, "Part on horses, part on women. The rest I spent foolishly."

WELCOME TO MY NEW COLLECTION

— £ —

I've started a new collection, one I can't believe anyone else has thought of—although you never know. Collectors are such strange, dopey people, inspired by such strange, dopey emotions and motives. Money is one, otherwise Sotheby's and Christie's would soon pack up. But it's only one reason why people collect.

Looking back regretfully, rather than forward hopefully, is the most common feeling for all collectors. We all wish we'd spotted certain things at the time, not chucked them out, or bought more when they were cheap. Oh, how often I have wished that I'd bought more houses in our street in 1964 when they were practically giving them away. Only £5,000 each, roll up. Such a shame that even saving the £1,400 deposit seemed to take forever.

I could easily have bought more Beatles concert programmes in the Sixties if only I'd known they'd be worth about £1,000 each today. Or Wembley programmes on July 30, 1966 for the World Cup final. I kept mine—it's now worth about £150—and my ticket stub. Nobody then collected tickets. I just thought it would look nice in my football collection. Now I've seen them on sale for £100.

I have about 20 collections on lots of daft topics: Beatrix Potter books, first editions of newspapers, prime ministers' autographs, suffragette postcards. I've got PM's back to Walpole, but have given up on suffragettes. The prices are now ridiculous. Most collectors start as accumulators, which means they don't throw out things that come their way. Then you wonder whether you can find more, add to, or complete the set. The notion of a 'set' is often in the mind of the collector, a self created list, but the thing being collected must in theory be finite or temporary. Otherwise, what's the point?

Apart from buying at auctions or junk shops or collectors' fairs for my existing collections, I am always starting new ones — ephemera of the day — which strike me as interesting, part of our times, a bit of modern social history. When the national lottery started in 1994, I made sure I bought a ticket on the first day. I didn't want to win, because of course I have enough money and a hard-working wife. Nor did I want to compete. I just wanted to have the ticket. It shows the date, Saturday November 19, 1994, and is stamped: First Day Issue. Ah, historic stuff. During that first year, I picked up Camelot's different leaflets whenever I was in a newsagent. I've still got them although I'm not sure where. At a rough reckoning, I would say the value today of my lottery collection is, let me see, using both fingers: nothing. But that's not the point. Collectors collect. We wait for the rest of the world to catch up with us.

My new collection is also at the moment completely valueless but awfully topical. We are at present in Lakeland for the summer season. The moment we arrived six weeks ago I became fascinated with all the foot-and-mouth notices. Some of the early ones politely announced a voluntary ban on walking on fields and fells. Then the notices became heavy with convoluted legalese as the situation grew worse. Most are issued by the National Park or Cumbria County Council. Some are printed by farm magazines, such as *Farmers' Guardian*. Some are pretty, with vignettes and a nice typeface. Some are scruffy and hand-written by farmers. I've managed to get hold of quite a few and taken photos of several others. I've made my farming neighbours promise to save stuff for me, not throw them out, once all this nastiness is over.

I'd be interested in buying a collection of foot-and-mouth memorabilia from 1967, if it exists, for at least a couple of quid, just to study the different notices, regulations, wording, layout. You don't realise how quickly such things date. My 2001 collection is not for money, just for my own interest. It is a record of the rural times I happen to be living through. That's why I'm trying to collect as many examples as possible, before it all disappears. Oh no. Just had a thought. If I am the first to think of it, there will now be others on the trail. Please eat this column after you have read it. Thanks.

The most expensive:

Mobile phone – $104,050
Made from 18-carat gold with a diamond-encrusted keypad. Designed by David Morris International, it was sold in 1996.

Washroom – $3.5 million
The toilet is made from 24-carat gold, the ceiling decorated with precious stones. Designed by jeweller Lam Sai-Wing.

Meal – £44,007
Spent by six diners at the London restaurant Petrus in 2001. The food cost £300, but the wine included a claret worth £12,300.

Perfume – $71,380
The four inch bottle of Parfum VI was designed by Arthur Burnham. Just 173 bottles were made.

Bra – $12.5 million
The Heavenly Star Bra was designed by Mouawad and is encrusted with sapphires and diamonds.

IT'S SPEND, SPEND, SPEND AFTER MY £30,000 FLUKE

— £ —

I don't do shares. No logical reasons. Just never fancied them. Don't like the idea of strangers having my money, then having to keep an eye on them. The hours and days some folks put in, watching the markets, moving their little piles around. How can they have time for other things in their lives, such as living?

Yes, I know if I'd put money into a good stock 30 years ago, closed my eyes and left it there, I'd be well pleased. So the experts say. And experts, looking back, are always right. Looking ahead, that's the bit they find dodgy. I also know that if you don't do stocks direct, you still can't avoid them. They come round the houses, in disguise, to haunt you. I've just got a letter from Northern Rock, a firm I've long favoured because of its name. What a combination, Northern and Rock. It's wasted on a boring old money firm. It should be a film star or a pop group. It has written about my Guaranteed Capital Bond, which I'd forgotten about. I knew how much money I had in it, but that was all. At the time, I must have been persuaded by the spiel — hurry, hurry, special offer, guaranteed not to fade. But the details had gone from my flibbertigibbetty mind.

Turns out the interest was tied to the FTSE index. On July 5, 1999, the index was 6,592. On July 5 this year, it had fallen to 5,549. The letter tells me I will therefore get no interest this year. Ha ha, Hunter. Got you there. For any queries ring the helpline and see if we care, see if we'll even answer before Christmas. Everywhere you look, it's much the same. Each day, another firm gives a profit warning. It must make them feel virtuous, warning people about something they can do bugger all about. You're half way across the river and someone shouts: "Crocodile. Oh, sorry, too late, but I did warn you."

All rates seem to be rubbish at the moment anyway, all returns negligible, so what is a poor investor to do. In this case, a rich investor. Yes I've just made a bit of a killing, oh yes. When I said I didn't do shares, that was a slight fib. In the 1980's, I did put £3,000 in those two start-up things for which there were tax advantages. One was to do with the Playhouse Theatre and dear Jeffrey Archer was involved. Almost at once, it collapsed. Never had a penny back. The other was for the Groucho Club. I put in £3,000 and recently have had up to £1,000 a year in dividends, plus a reduced membership as a founder shareholder. Clever old me. Even more remarkable is what's now happened. Last month, the club was taken over and my £3,000 has turned out to be worth about £30,000. I say about because I've taken part in loan notes, whatever they are. I can't quite read the small print.

So, on reflection, I should now swallow my words about shares. But I won't. Investing in the Groucho Club was a fluke, a one-off. But what am I going to do with the £30,000? Suggestions on a blank cheque please. Buy better specs? That would be a start. Invest in a proper filing system or a computer? That would be sensible. I could then quickly look up the details of whatever other nonsenses Northern Rock has sold me.

Looking around, scanning all the alluring adverts, I can see nothing tempting. What I like best are guaranteed returns, and they're all lousy. So at present I'm not going to invest in the financial sector, or similar. Property? That's still the best but £30,000 wouldn't buy me a garage in Hampstead. Leave it in the bank? What, and get a measly ooo.1% interest. All HSBC seems to do with my money is spend it on thick, glossy booklets telling me that this week I now have a Premier account, not to be confused with the booklet sent last week about the Meridian account.

Leave it under the bed? You're getting warmer. Inflation will reduce it but not a lot. Just think what you'll save not having any paperwork or hanging on for customer services. Spend, spend, spend? That's for me. And for millions like me, judging by the fact that consumer spending is booming. You can't take anything with you, as the crocodile said to the man in the river ...

The famous board game Monopoly was invented by an unemployed Pennsylvanian man, Charles Darrow, in 1934. When he failed to sell his idea to Parker Brothers, but remained convinced that the game would bring him fame and fortune, he made his sets by hand. Such was its success that Parker Brothers changed their minds and in 1935 Monopoly became the best selling game in the States.

At least, that's the official version.

But the original idea came from political economist Lizzie Magie who in 1904 patented 'The Landlord's Game'. Magie, a Quaker from Virginia, was part of a tax movement led by Henry George. She devised the game as away to teach the single tax theory — the idea that taxes should be based on the amount of land a person owned. When she tried to sell the rights to the game to George Parker, it was rejected as too political. Today Monopoly has been translated into 26 languages, including Braille.

— £ —

I'm sitting waiting for the postie. Here in Lakeland he comes mid-morning, about three hours later than in London. But at least when he comes he takes our letters away and we also have a good chat. Rural postmen and women become friends, part of the community. There used to be one who had a cup of tea at each farmhouse, did little jobs for the elderly, even cut their grass. He got the sack in the end. Some mean person complained when their post wasn't arriving till after it was dark.

I am waiting to hear from Ernie. Three months without a sausage. It's the longest ever wait. I do so look forward to seeing the familiar letter from Blackpool, tearing open the envelope, looking for that neat slip that proves he still loves me. 'Dear Bondholder'. That's how he always refers to me. A bit impersonal, considering how long we have known each other, but it's the next word that matters: 'Congratulations'.

My wife and I have had the maximum possible invested in premium bonds since 1998. I can still remember the excitement of that day in October 1999 when I won £1,000. You feel so clever, so smart. Big lottery winners feel the same, convincing themselves they've earned it, deserved it. After that, nowt, or almost nowt. Just a lot of boring £50 wins. The annual totals, as you've asked, for an outlay of £40,000, are £1,600 in 1998; £2,500 in 1999, because of that big one; and £1,200 in 2000. That represents an average return of just over 4%, which is pretty good. This year, though, we've only won £700. It could turn out to be my worst year yet.

The National Savings people have recently been spending a lot of money, my money of course, on huge newspaper ads which ask: 'Will you be celebrating a £1m win in August?' It's very enticing, until you read the small print at the bottom where it says that from September, the interest rate on which the prize fund is calculated will be 'changed from 3.75% to 3.5%'. Note the weasely use of the word 'changed'. What they mean is 'reduced'. If the change had been upwards, they wouldn't have said 'changed'. They would have screamed 'increased'.

Have you ever met anyone who has won a million on the premium bonds? Or even read about them? Nor me. Yet they guarantee there is a new millionaire every month. I held this promise out to my two grandchildren, Amelia and Ruby, not that they understood it, being one day old at the time. I gave them £1,000 each in premium bonds on their birthday. I told Ruby, who lives in Botswana, that when she gets to 16 she can come to London and live it up by which time her £1,000 should be worth double, if not millions. Ruby is now 20 months old—and has won nothing. Amelia, who lives in Tufnell Park, is two and a quarter and has won £50.

The post has come. No sign of the million. Not even a measly £50. I think I'll cash in and put the money into, well er, what? Where can you invest that's guaranteed, tax free and secure? The answer is National Savings certificates. I have moaned about them for years. Waste of time, what a con. But I have just looked at their rates and they are not bad, considering that rates everywhere are rubbish. Fixed-rates certificates went up on July 19. They now pay 3.8% tax free, which works out at 6.33% for higher-rate taxpayers. That's better than most banks and building societies. I might well give it a go. For old times sake.

I have had savings certificates all my life. Most people had them when I was a lad. I can remember my mother in the 1940s giving me a half-crown each Monday to take to school to buy savings stamps which you stuck in a little book. Wasn't that a brilliant bit of marketing? Why can't they do it today?

Today's teachers would probably go spare. In that case, pay them a fee to collect the money. Are you listening, Gordon Brown? When lovely Sarah gives birth, you will no doubt buy baby Brown some savings certificates or premium bonds. At the same time, why not re-introduce them into schools? The point about premium bonds and savings certificates is not just their tax-freeness. You don't declare them, so there's no paperwork. That's a huge attraction. My ambition in life is to have my financial affairs so arranged that I no longer need an accountant. He would then have to go and find a proper job. The other attraction is feeling virtuous because you are helping the government, letting it play with your money, even if all it does is spend it on potty advertisements.

I think all people with National Savings certificates should automatically get an OBE for services to the country. As for people like me, with the maximum in premium bonds, who don't win the million, I think the least we can expect is a life peerage. Thank you, Tony.

"There are few ways in which a man can be more innocently employed than in getting money."
Samuel Johnson

"The love of money is the root of all evil."
The Bible
(First Epistle of Paul to Timothy)

CAN'T WAIT, WON'T WAIT

— £ —

The world divides into those who want it now, and will pay for it, and those prepared to wait. It doesn't seem to matter how well-off people are. Rich or poorish, middling affluent or seriously loaded, the divide is still there. It's an emotional, spiritual, perhaps even genetic difference — one which we don't seem able to do anything about. Some people just seem to need instant satisfaction, to hold and touch, see and examine, and they are not prepared to wait. But there are others who can control themselves, contain their excitement, hang on a few more hours, perhaps days, or weeks if the post is dodgy.

I am of course talking photographs. I can never understand those folks who see the sign, 'Your Prints Developed in One Hour, Price a Fortune'. Any sensible person, such as myself, knows that if you are prepared to wait a day or three, you'll only have to pay half a fortune.

My three children, who are not at all well off — though they will be one day I hope and keep me in my old age, or what's left of it — always rush back from their summer hols and get their pictures instantly developed. I could easily afford to do the same, could buy my own photographic shop, make a take-over bid for Kodak, yet I would never for one moment consider paying extra for photographic speed. Potty, I call it.

It so happens that I have two rolls of film of our summer here in Lakeland to be developed. They're mainly of me and my dear wife in the garden, standing or sitting beside our wrought iron peacock. I take that one every year. There's also some longer shots with Grasmoor and Mellbreak fells looming over us. Plus Crummock Water, twinkling in the distance. Another favourite.

So what's the hurry to get them printed? I also know roughly how they'll all turn out. Several will have funny yellow-orangey blobs while others will appear to show nothing at all, thanks to trying to catch our resident family of red squirrels through the conservatory window, in the rain, while they were still miles away, or perhaps not there at all.

Last week, while in Carlisle, I went into Boots in English Street and asked how much. For 24 standard size, done in an hour, the price was £6.99. But if I was prepared to wait six days, so I was told, the price would then drop to £2.99. That's more like it. "How about," I said to the assistant. "If I was prepared to wait 12 days, would you do them for £1.99?"

"You what?"

"Or say I was willing to hang on till next year, or longer, till I was gone, so you could send them to me posthumously. Presumably you would then do them for free?"

"Good try," he said. "But no."

So I brought them home, undeveloped, waiting for a sign from heaven or a special offer through the post. My wife said how silly, how mean, but just typical. It's true. I would never for example pay for same-day dry cleaning, preferring to wait longer and get it cheaper. I can't actually remember when I last had anything dry cleaned. I like to believe that Oxfam always does it first, so there's no need. I would never pay extra and get a taxi if I could get a bus, even though it would be quicker. Actually, that's not true any more. Not in London. Taxis and buses both take forever.

I go mad when I find my wife has put a first class stamp on a boring letter to a fan. She says it's taken weeks to get here, via publisher and agent, so it's only fair to reply quickly. I scream even louder. "It's a con, the whole thing's a con. First is no faster than second." Then I have to lie down.

If I was a young woman, would I lash out and buy a pregnancy test kit, which you see them doing all the time, so I would know in an hour if I was up the duff? Or would I hang on, wait a few months, save my pennies, till I could feel it kicking? Hmm, that would be a hard decision. Even for me.

I can lash out on big expenditures. If I think that's the price, and I want it, but I get a blockage in my mind when it comes to paying extra for speed when speed doesn't really matter. In fact I quite enjoy waiting. As a child, I saved the best bits on the plate till last. When my mother gave us a banana each, I always waited till my brother and sisters had eaten theirs before I ate mine, just to make them jealous. Do I need therapy?

Anyway, I came home and found a special offer had arrived. From Bonusprint. Up to 27 prints, regular size, only £1.99. I know 'regular' size could mean postage stamp size, and I might not see them till Christmas, but come on, I will have saved another fortune.

Well fancy giving money to the Government!
    Might as well put it down the drain
Fancy giving money to the Government
    Nobody will see the stuff again
They've no idea what money's for
    Ten to one they'll start another war
I've heard a lot of silly things, but Lor!
    Fancy giving money to the Government

    – A.P. Herbert

MONEY IS BEST LEFT UNDER THE BED

— £ —

The Equitable Life affair, about which I'm still not talking, has been so depressing that I decided to do something totally different and out of character. It was my own fault, putting all our pension savings into Equitable Life, instead of spreading them around. Even dafter, in 1998 when I started drawing the annuity, I put it all into a maximum investment plan—with Equitable Life. I'm still being punished twice for my stupidity. Which I'm not talking about.

Anyway the only bright moment, with regard to the company I won't mention, has been its bright purple bumper bundle sent out to all its suckers. For a company with no money it is amazing that it can splash out on 90-odd pages of thick, glossy paper, complete with high-class envelope and folders. I do admire the firm. At times like this, who wants cheap printing? I carefully cut out all the blank glossy pages, and the pretty folder cover, and now have a stash of free classy paper which I plan to re-use for Christmas cards. Thanks, chaps. I also amused myself by filling in the comments card on equally pretty purple paper.

No.8 asked for any other options that should be

considered. "Give us back our money and close the company," I wrote. Quite cheered me up. The out-of-character thing I did, in the middle of all this mess, happened on August 14.

I was walking down Main Street in Cockermouth, Cumbria, when I decided to go into the Midland Bank. It will always be the Midland to me. I said I wanted to buy some shares. It came as a surprise to me to hear these words coming out of my mouth. I've always been against shares. But I had a £20,000 Bristol & West bond that was due to mature. It was quite a surprise for the Midland as well. I don't think people normally walk in off Main Street and ask to buy shares. It is quite a small branch. There was some whispering, lights were put on in a back room and I sat down with a nice young man in a suit who admitted he was not used to doing this. Me neither, I said. I sucked my pencil hard, studied the FTSE 100, and chose four shares, pretty much at random.

We shall always have to eat, so I picked Safeway. I shall always be drinking, so that means Scottish & Newcastle. I shall always need petrol, so I shall take BP. And people will always use money, but which company? There was a notice saying HSBC, whatever that means—oh yeah, it's the Midland, so I'll have some of that.

Those are the four shares I invested in on August 15. Look, please don't jump ahead. I know you know what is going to happen but just contain yourselves. I bought

HSBC at 840p. Almost immediately it fell, dropping by more than 25% to 608p on September 24. As I write, it is up in the 700s, but it is still a hell of a big climb back. Scottish & Newcastle was 529p. Last week it was 525p, so that is not good. Safeway was 360p and is now 329p. I got BP at 600p and last time I looked it was down to 594p. Good timing, huh? Having waited a lifetime to buy shares, I chose now. I could have picked any time in the past 30 years, but I had to do it just before September 11.

With the shares, I am in for the long haul, so that is fortunate. I hope, touch wood, I shall not need to sell for years. The fall in the share prices serves me right for being greedy, gambling in the hope of a good profit, instead of doing what any sensible person should be doing in these hard times: either spending the cash or leaving it under the bed. But it has provided me with a new activity. Not having had shares before, I have never been aware of prices. Now it is the third thing I check each morning. I look first at the Premier League — I do have my priorities right — where Spurs are falling fast. Next, I check the Third Division table, where Carlisle United have already dropped to the bottom. Then the FT thingy, to see my shares.

I now have three things to follow, all doing appallingly but they have to be watched in case of any dramatic improvements. So, something good has come out of all this bad news, along with the purple paper.

The largest credit card collection is owned
by Walter Cavanagh of California.
Number of cards: 1397
Worth: $1.65 million
Cost: Nil

PHONEY PHONES

— £ —

I am the resident meanie in this house, the one who goes
around switching lights off, screams at people for using
first class stamps, eats up leftovers even if it's stuff I hate,
buys only bargains or seconds and always tries to shop at
Oxfam. Correction: except the one in Carlisle.

I went into Carlisle's Oxfam the other week to look at
the cheapo second-hand books and spotted a nice looking 1936 edition of Ibsen's *Peer Gynt* illustrated by
Arthur Rackham. The dozy women volunteers won't
know its value, I thought. I'll probably get it for a couple
of bob. I opened it and saw the price — £274.99. Oxfam?

Yes, I couldn't believe it. Nor why with such a big price they'd bothered to add the piddling 99p at the end. That's Oxfam off my list when I go looking for Christmas presents.

Nobody pulls a fast one on Hunt. They don't catch him out. Well, except Equitable Life, but we're not talking about that. Or Marks and Spencer. Just had a letter from M&S to tell me my Pep, which was worth £11,418 on April 6, is now worth only £10,488. But it was polite. The covering letter says: 'Thank you for your continued investment with us.' Wasn't that thoughtful. Oh, and Scottish Widows. Also very well brought up when it comes to communication. It has kindly written to inform me that my with-profits thing is now subject to a market level adjustment and also a current surrender value. It means my investment is now worth £2,700 less than it was half an hour ago. So it goes. Gone.

Look after the pennies, I always told my children, and the pounds will take care of themselves. While I might be coming a cropper on the big scene, with all my investments turning out rubbish, just like everyone else's, at home, chez moi, I am still master of my fate, captain of my soul, nobody takes me for a ride.

Then our phone started playing up. People could ring in but we couldn't ring out. I contacted BT and was told how to test it. We have three phones on the same line. BT said if the Tribune phone was faulty, someone would come and repair it. But if it was one of the other two, there would be a £60 charge. After a couple of hours, it righted itself, so I didn't need an engineer but I was still puzzled by the Tribune thing, so I rang to get it explained. "It's the one you rent from BT." Oh no I don't, I said. I'm not that daft, you don't catch me. But they had. Thanks to my own stupidity and ignorance and not reading the small print properly on the BT bills, I've been paying rental of £4.46 a quarter for, I dunno, probably 15 years. It might have seemed reasonable 15 years ago but now you can buy cheapo phones anywhere.

I went out the next day and got a brand new phone at Dixons for £6.99. What a bargain. And it works perfectly. Yet I've been paying £17.84 a year to rent something I could have got for well under half of that. I must have wasted about a couple of hundred pounds. Okay, so BT would have repaired it free, big deal. But at £6.99, I can afford to buy two new ones every year, if they go wrong, and still be quids in. The Tribune phone has now gone back to BT, post-free — they didn't catch me on that. But I haven't told anyone else in this house about it. I have this reputation to maintain. Am I not the smart one? Am I not the one who tells everyone else off for wasting money? Am I not the one who has always said take care of the pennies? That was then. In future, I'm no longer going to say it. Traditionally, it did work, did make sense.

Bit by bit, savers who saved small and steadily, were careful and prudent, did eventually get themselves a nice little pile at the end. Not in these hard financial times. Big sums or small sums, out of nowhere there can appear politely printed, weasely worded circulars informing you that market value reductions are being made, so, ha ha, you've been had, sucker.

The piece of financial wisdom I intend to pass on to my grandchildren is very simple, though it's taken a lifetime to learn it. Whether it's big money or small money, the best thing to do is spend, spend, spend.

Easy ways to make money:

Surveys – earn cash or vouchers for completing surveys.

Medical trials – earn up to £100 a day to test a new pill or jab.

Football stewards – earn £5–£10 an hour on match day as a part-time steward.

Give blood – earn around £60 for 600ml of blood, used for scientific testing.

Give sperm – earn about £25 for each donation, but you have to be under 40 and fit.

ID parade – earn £15 for taking part in a police ID parade.

I'VE PAID MY TAXES, SO NOW I'LL
USE THE BUS PASS

— £ —

I'm 65. I don't mind admitting it. In fact I've been looking forward to it for the past five years. It is utterly
appalling and disgraceful, not to mention sexist, that
women get their passes at 60 while men have to wait
until 65. They live longer than us so, if anything, we
should have our old-age concessions at 60, not them.
'Snot fair. Now I'm always on the bus, hopping on and
off, changing after one stop if I don't like the driver or
the passengers. I could afford to pay, or go by taxi, but
there's nothing as enjoyable in this life as free things.

I remember sitting with John Lennon at his home
when some presents and gifts arrived from people and
firms he didn't know. His enjoyment was childlike,
ripping open the parcels. When the Beatles were poor,
they had to pay for everything. Once they could buy
anything, they didn't have to. The economics of being
wealthy throws the theory of economics up in the air. My
wife, who is younger than me, has been enjoying her bus
pass for three years now. Which is strange. She has gone
through life refusing free things, ignoring special offers,
never taking two when they are the price of one. I've

seen the staff at supermarket check-outs pointing out the offers to her, even saying they'll go and get her the free one. But she still says no, thank you. I'm talking Cockermouth or Carlisle. In a London supermarket, you'd get a punch in the gob if you did anything to hold up the queue.

When our three children were small, she refused for years to claim our family allowance. It began when she saw a photograph of Lord Montgomery, I think, queuing for his old-age pension. She thought it awful that he should be claiming when he clearly did not need it. I agreed with her and felt frightfully virtuous until one day I discovered that my accountant was filling in my tax forms as if we had been getting the family allowance. So I stopped all that nonsense.

I have an interesting conversation with myself whenever I go 'up street', as we call the West End in our house. I go on the bus — or sequence of buses — to have lunch with a chum or do a little job, but I've always walked back. I can get home from Broadcasting House in 55 minutes flat, or 75 minutes if I take the scenic route. Now, of course, I can ride home free, which I point out to myself. So far I've resisted this temptation. There you are, pet. She always says I'm a sucker for anything free. I've had a senior-citizen rail card for five years which gives me a discount on train tickets. You have to pay for it, and I don't use the railways enough, so I think I'll give it up.

The other week I was at the doctor's and saw this notice addressed to the 'elderly'. It turned out to mean the over 65s, cheeky sods, who were entitled to a free flu jab. Never had one before, but it was free. Felt lousy ever since. Is it a judgement? Or an attempt to finish off the elderly and save money on beds?

I discovered last week another advantage of being 65. I brought back by mistake a book from Carlisle Library and forgot about it until I got a £14 bill for it being over-due. Did I scream and moan—and at the postage, which was £3. Yesterday they sent me another letter. "I am returning your cheque as OAPs do not pay fines." I never knew that but it was the best news of the day. Fair cheered me up.

In cinemas, I don't ask if they do senior-citizen discounts, not if there are other people in the queue. Why draw attention to oneself? Okay, it's vanity. I like to pretend that nobody for one moment would take me for 65.

There are lots of firms offering discounts on home and car insurance for oldies but I've never knowingly been attracted to them. There's such competition in the insurance field anyway that it gives me a headache just trying to compare prices.

At 65, I'm now due my full old-age pension from the state, unlike my wife. They did write to her at 60, saying she would qualify for 14p a week. Something to do with not having worked, or not paid her full National

Insurance rates. I didn't bother to work it out, or fill in the forms, or even tell her. So she can still feel virtuous. But I'm taking my pension, oh yes, and paying higher-rate tax on it, so the government is getting 40% of my money back. And of course it is my money.

I once interviewed Sir Alan Sugar and above his desk he had a framed cheque to the Inland Revenue dated March 27, 1989 for £48,231,250. I haven't quite paid that amount but over 43 years of working, it's mounting up. I consider my bus pass is not in fact free. I've paid for it.

Some jolly useful savings tips:

1. Use your local library — to get free books and to order any title you want. Mobile libraries usually have no overdue charges. Pensioners can rent videos free.
2. Use second hand bookshops, charity shops, jumble sales, discount bookshops.
3. Read a newspaper online for free.

Personal care saving tips:

1. Do your own haircuts.
2. Buy supermarket own brands of cosmetics and toiletries.

Christmas savings tips:

1. Shop early during the sales.
2. Compare prices — the website Dealtime UK does this.
3. Make your own presents, like sweets.
4. Buy cards in the January sales or summer clearances, or make your own.

CHAPTER FOUR

Isas, Tessas, and other girls

— £ —

SWIM PROVES I SPLASH OUT

Nobody can say I'm mean with money. I fritter it away all the time, all over the place. Why, the other day I spent £333 just to have a swim. It was Sunday morning and, as ever, I went swimming at Kentish Town baths. For the first time for years I drove there because I was going on to Bloomsbury to a book fair and a postcard fair, both on the same day, in the same hotel. Gosh, I was really excited.

I parked outside the baths on a single yellow line. Early Sunday morning, no problem. When I came out half an hour later, my car had gone. Oh God. I went round to the police station in Holmes Road and said: "Quick, my car has been nicked, put out a call at once and you'll catch the kid who's pinched it. It's a Jag, with my initials on, very easy to spot." The cop on duty refused. He said I needed my driving licence and log book to prove I owned it, before they could put out a call. "Ring the DVLA people in Swansea," I said. "You'll see I am the owner. And look, I've got proof of who I am: this BBC pass with my photo on." (Ten years old, but I kept my finger over the date.) He still refused. I ranted and raved, asked whose side he was on — he's supposed to help catch villains, not help them escape.

I ran home, got my documents, came back and by now there was a huge queue with other people who'd had their cars nicked. This dopey policeman was taking forever. When it was my turn, he said he'd just check the compound to make sure my car hadn't been towed away. "Don't be daft," I said. "Sunday morning, single yellow, only there half an hour. Don't waste even more time."

But he was right and I had to apologise profusely. I rang my daughter — still in bed, so she wasn't best pleased — to come and drive me to the compound. When we got to the gates, I thanked her and sent her away, telling her to go back to bed. What a mistake! When I got inside and had to pay £155 to get my car released, it turned out to have a flat tyre. It had been perfect when I'd left it and recently serviced. So more ranting and raving. I blamed the clamping people for bursting the tyre when lifting it into their truck. Which, of course, they denied. I couldn't drive it away, but if I didn't, I'd be charged storage. I don't do tyre changing so

I walked miles to a garage and asked for a mechanic to help. But it was Sunday and they didn't have one. Instead they sold me, for £6, a can of instant mending stuff. It worked and the tyre went up.

On the way home, I went into a Kwik-Fit and asked them to check the tyre. They said it could not be repaired because I'd used this can of stuff. I needed a new tyre, price £172. Gawd, I'm getting a headache just going over the saga. But that's how my swim cost £333.

It's happened to all of us, being penalised for parking, but it's only the second time in 40 years I've been towed away. And as usual it happens when you least expect it, when your mind is miles away, when you are busy planning other things. And the pain, the hellish pain, of spending all that money, and getting bugger all in return. I lost three hours of my life, ranting and moaning, and had to go and lie down for the rest of the afternoon. I tried to console myself with the fact that I had not gone to the two Bloomsbury fairs and so had saved money. My other consolatory thought is that when you spend money on self-indulgence you receive benefits. The moral is therefore to enjoy it, not count the cost. For very soon, friends, there will be more money unexpectedly flowing down the drain. (Yes, I am thinking of you, Mr Equitable.)

"Money is welcome though it come in a dirty clout."
– 1629, *Howell's Collections of Proverbs*

"Muck and money go together."
– 1678, J. Ray, *English Proverbs*

And a variation on the above, though not quite as cynical:
"Money is like muck, not good except it be spread."
– Francis Bacon

HAPPINESS IS A DOGGY BAG
AT 30,000 FEET

— £ —

Ever since 1986 I've gone through life Club class. It was
the year I turned 50 and went wild, treating myself to the
West Indies for the first time. From then on, I ceased to
be an economy person, the sort who goes everywhere
cheapo. I am not yet a first class fellow. I can't quite rise
to that, emotionally or spiritually, not while I'm still me,
in this skin — which, yes, is pretty brown just now, glad
you noticed.

I didn't plan it that way. The 1986 trip was going to be a one-off, but my dear wife said: "That's it, it has to be Club from now on or I'm not going anywhere. I'll stay at home and you can go on your own, as you've always said there's no difference between Club and economy." Which is true, in most ways. The Club class bit of the plane gets there no more quickly than economy. The noise of the bloody engine is just the same. In a crash, Clubbers and firsts are no safer than those at the back of the plane. So why pay about three times as much when all you get is a bit more space and a few fripperies?

And yet, do you know, I've grown quite accustomed to its face. With age, it is a great help to have that bit more legroom and be able to lie flattish when trying to sleep. And like all mean people, I greatly enjoy all the rubbish, I mean treasures, you are given. Those free toilet bags make wonderful presents for deprived people back home, such as my children, who have not been able to afford a Caribbean hol, bless them. Very often, though, I have decided that the little tube of lip gel, miniature moisturiser or free socks would be wasted on my children. Which is how I come to have at the back of the wardrobe a dozen vintage Club class toilet bags. I must clear out the mouldy ones—could be a health hazard by now.

I take the socks to Lakeland and wear them there, although they don't last long—rubbish material. The eyeshades are always a problem. Even on the plane, I never know how to put them on or what to do with the two stupid bits of string. It's like going to sleep with a pair of knickers on your head. It's strange, really, that I've enjoyed receiving all this junk, when of course I know that I'm paying £2,000 extra to get about £20 worth of tat. But I'm also getting Club service which I have to say has generally been excellent. And you do get that little glow of unjustified pride that spending too much money can bring. You feel a better class of person when you use a better class of crockery, drink a better glass of wine or plonk your bum in a better class of lounge. It's nonsense of course, a con trick on one's vanity, when you think how much you pay for this. Yet for 16 years I've indulged myself.

On my last flight home from Barbados I began to wonder if I would remain a Club class person. It used to be so cosy on a plane with just a handful of Club class people upstairs. Now it always seems to be so full and noisy. We got plastic cutlery, ugh, although we all know why. But I couldn't find the reason why we were given no menu and little choice of food. All gone, they said, when they finally reached us, only fish or salad left. After we complained, they did find some meat, left over from first class. Lucky us. In economy, they were probably on stewed sick bags. But, worst of all, no doggy bag was given out, so I didn't get my useless miniature toothpaste or stupid plastic comb. What a swiz. Presumably another economy.

I've just rung BA, which confirmed that it doesn't give out 'amenity kits' any more. Instead, you have to ask for them. So they say. I will, of course, go BA Club again. Too late to revert. But it's a good job I've got that stash in the wardrobe. I'll be able to take my own doggy bag with me next time.

Joseph Addison, the 18th Century essayist and co-founder of *The Spectator*, had a friend with whom he used to conduct long and heated arguments on topics of the day — until the friend borrowed some money from him. From then on, the friend agreed with absolutely everything Addison said. In the end, Addison got so fed up that when his friend nodded in agreement on a point which Addison knew that previously his friend had taken the total contrary view, he shouted at him: "Either contradict me, sir, or pay me my money back."

I'M NOT TIGHT, BUT YOU
CAN'T BEAT A DISCOUNT

— £ —

You'd have thought someone tight with money — no, I'm not thinking of anyone in particular — would know the price of things. You'd have thought someone out and about, mixing with the masses, riding the buses, gaping in shop windows, going to jumbles, looking for bargains — yes, now I'm thinking of me — would know what basic items cost these days.

"And while you're at the shop, get a bottle of milk," said my wife as I went off to buy an evening paper.

"Oh no," I said, groaning.

"Too much for you to remember, is it? Should I write it down?"

It wasn't that. It was because I'd just counted out the money for the evening paper and had it exact, all in change.

I've found this stash of money upstairs, in pennies or similar, mostly still current currency, left over by our son when he left home. Whenever he was going out, he emptied his pocket of small change, not wanting to weigh down his lovely clothes, and just dumped it at the back of a drawer. I found it a month ago and have been going through it steadily. It is perfect for the evening paper, though the newsagent moans when there's a queue and he's got to count it all out, which he always does, suspiciously. I hate tight people.

"How much will it be?" I asked.

"You don't know the price of milk? I am surprised. I thought you knew the price of everything," my wife said.

I stormed out, feeling sorry for those politicians who get caught out at elections when they don't know the price of a pint of beer and get ridiculed for being out of touch or too rich. I like to think I'm neither but in fact I don't know the price of beer. Could it be £1, £2, or £3? I don't go in pubs or drink beer. I don't know the price of milk. It comes to the door every morning, in the dark, so you never see the cow. We pay the milkman by cheque, once every couple of months but I never actually look at the unit cost. Could it be 30p or 60p? It's in a bottle, but is it pints? Gawd, I don't even know that.

A cynic, so they say, knows the price of everything and the value of nothing, which personally I think is cobblers. It doesn't actually work that way. All of us, rich and poor, careful and spendthrift, are an amalgam. We all have blind spots, prices for some reason we are unaware of, because we don't buy the goods, and prices we don't know because we don't care — we'll buy those items regardless. Toothpaste: I have no idea how much toothpaste costs but in a supermarket I will pick up the brand we normally buy without looking at the price.

I was at the supermarket yesterday and bought 48 bottles of Safeway's Beaujolais, our favourite, which should keep me and the missus going until we go to Lakeland in May. I don't know the price of Safeway's Beaujolais. I don't care, I'll get it regardless. But I know the discount: 5% off per dozen. After that I filled the car with petrol, also at Safeway. I have no idea of the price of the petrol. All I know is that you get 5p off per litre if you spend more than £40. Sometimes the discount has been 10p a litre, which is brilliant. But it is run like Russian roulette — the discount is suddenly announced, with no advance warning, then whipped off again, the rotters. I do find myself attracted by discounts, while being unaware of the price, which is mad, but I'm sure millions do the same. They don't take me in with 'Sale' notices, or 'Closing down' or 'All stock must go'. I'm too wise for that, always suspecting that the stuff will probably be rubbish.

But when I see 'Discount' on wine or petrol, which I'm going to buy anyway, I'll rush, slavering, let me pass, I'm almost a doctor. On big one-off expenditures, as opposed to regular provisions, I know exactly what I spend, and I will haggle every pound, get the price down, as I did with my car. I bought that second-hand last year for, er, oh no, the awful thing is, I now can't remember what I paid. Was it £10,000 or £12,000? And what did I get for the old one? Appalling, yet it mattered so much at the time. The point is, knowing or not knowing prices doesn't mean you are mean, or not mean — I don't in fact know what it means. But I now know the price of milk and that my wife doesn't know the price of the evening paper. I asked her when I got back and she guessed 45p. Huh. So much for mocking me.

The answers, for those making notes: This week in March 2002 the London Evening Standard costs 35p. The cheapest beer at our local, Adnams, is £2.10 a pint. Milk at our nearest shop is 38p a pint. Delivered to our door by Mr Milson it's 40p and comes in a glass bottle, which gets recycled, thus saving the world. Thank you. I like to think this is a column of record.

Celebrities who went bankrupt:

- Former footballer George Best, bankrupt in 1982 owing £22,000.
- Former rock star Gary Glitter, bankrupt in 1980, owed the Inland Revenue £170,000 and the Fulham Road Tandoori £60.
- Clarissa Dickson-Wright, of the *Two Fat Ladies* TV cookery show, bankrupt in 1975 apparently due to the champagne bill at her mother's funeral. Also declared bankrupt in 1982 and 2003.

BUY ONE, GET ADDICTED FOR FREE

— £ —

Sainsbury's has opened in Cockermouth, so this small town now has a big shop.

"I'm not going to patronise it," said my wife. "I'll stick with Walter Willson."

"Suit yourself," I said.

Walter Willson is a small-time chain of ancient Cumbrian grocery stores. Above my desk in Lakeland, as I write, I have a 1920s photograph of a Walter Willson store in Aspatria. You don't know where that is, but don't worry. A sign over this 1920s shop, situated in a remote Cumberland village, boasts in large letters: 'Shops everywhere'. It does make me smile but I am easily amused. It suggests they had branches in London, Paris, New York and Outer Mongolia. In real life I should think they never got further than Penrith.

My wife likes Walter Willson's. It's always empty and the staff are charming. But you know how it is: one day she wanted a big shop, some exotic items, and off we went to try out the new super Sainsbury's. When we'd unpacked and I was putting something in the waste bin, I saw a coupon that offered £3 off for every £30 spent, and a leaflet about a Sainsbury's reward card. I fished them out—quite a messy business as I think we had eaten fish that evening—and said: "Look, petal, you've thrown out these great offers."

"Total rubbish," she said. "I don't want them."

So I filled them in, in her name, as she is officer in charge of provisions. Next time we went to Sainsbury's, I picked up her reward card. As she was paying, I shoved it over the till. Guess what? Not only did she get reward points, she got a scratch card. She rubbed it and found she had won a bottle of Diet Coke. Wow.

"I'm not having that in my house," she said. "Horrible stuff."

Yes, but we might have poor people visiting. I'm told some of them quite like Diet Coke. So I took it home. Next visit, she won a tin of Heinz chopped tomatoes.

"They're no use to me," she said. "I only use Italian chopped tomatoes."

Unlike her, I love free things. I never ring those winning numbers you get through the post that promise you a free prize, because I know the phone call will cost a fortune. I don't play the lottery or buy scratch cards, because you have to buy a ticket. But when it's part of a dopey promotional scheme, and all free, why not take part? Well-off people love free things and of course the weller-off you are, the more you get free. Millionaire footballers pay for nothing. And the professional middle classes are just as keen on anything that is free or offers a discount.

"But it's never free," says my wife. "You pay in the end."

Oh, she's so wise. She'd be more impressed if they lowered prices all round rather than pretend something is free. When I studied the small print, it explained how you got a free scratch card for every £25 spent. That sounded free enough. I then discovered that among the prizes was a Peugeot 307 LX 1.4. No idea what that is, just as you have no idea where Aspatria is, but I got the message: a free car.

"You're on a roll," I said. "Only two scratch cards so far and you've won a prize each time. You could win the big one next time we go to Cockermouth. In fact, can't we go now? I know we don't need to stock up again just yet, but surely there is £25 of basic stuff we could do with, just in case."

"If I win a car on my scratch card, I will turn to the next person in the queue behind me and give it to him or her," she said.

"You what? Don't be potty. You're winding me up."

"And next time I do go, I am going alone. I don't want you with me. Is that clear?"

I've got a false beard and even scruffier clothes than I usually wear, hidden in the boot of the car. Next time we're in Cockermouth, I'll put them on and lurk behind her in the queue at Sainsbury's. When she turns round, with her winning scratch card, I'll look ever so deserving and ever so grateful. Then I'll grab it and run.

"Money makes a man free." – 1542

"Money makes the man."
– Also first spotted in 1542.

CHARITY BEGINS AT SPURS

— £ —

My wife was on the phone when I came into my room. She was holding on for somebody at the other end, listening to some stupid music. I know what it's like. I do most of our business calls and it drives me mad. Getting through to a human voice at HSBC or Northern Rock or British Telecom—God, they put you through it. They ask for passwords and special dates, so special that I can't remember them. They offer options, none of which you want, or repeat the same tune until you scream. Or hang up.

It was taking ages so I hoped she was on a freephone number and certainly not being conned into ringing some dopey premium line. But I said nowt. I know my place. I went into the conservatory and sat down. She can't cope with people talking while she's on the phone—one of the penalties of never having worked in an office. I heard her give her Visa card number and say, yes, £100, that's what I'd like to give, thank you, ever so sweetly, knowing I was listening, tight lipped, tight-fisted, in the conservatory.

"It's my money," she shouted from the stairs, on the way up to work in her own little room.

There had been an advert in the newspaper that morning, calling for help for the starving in Afghanistan or it might have been Ethiopia. I knew when I saw it what would happen. I should have hidden the paper before she saw it. I won't know precisely what it's for until the Visa bills come in. I pay them from our joint account, the only one we have. Even then, it won't necessarily be clear. When she responds to a radio appeal, they often give a box number and a name that doesn't mean much. And often she can't remember, either.

Don't you find that friends, human beings, on the whole, divide into those who are spontaneously generous and those, er, who are not? She will give to beggars or buskers in the street, make a donation on entering a church or museum when it clearly says it is voluntary and respond to almost any worthy cause. Well done, her. I hold back, suspecting the beggar will spend it on booze or drugs or that the worthy cause or museum has people swanning off round the world enjoying themselves.

"I'm not giving to him," I'll say. "He's smoking a cigarette. If he can afford fags, he can't be all that hard up. And look, he's got a dog."

I'd never give to animal charities of any sort or political parties. I was incensed once when somebody tried to get £500 out of me for a Labour lunch, saying I might sit next to a Labour nob. Roy Hattersley, it might have been. I do pay Labour Party subs at the minimum rate but refuse to contribute more than that. I don't want them spending my money on daft posters.

With my wife, it's an immediate emotional response. I'm unable to do that, thinking of where the money might go. It's really nothing to do with meanness. Well, not everything. I can be calculatedly generous, as opposed to spontaneous. Over the years, I have contributed to various concerns, such as Amnesty International and Marie Curie Cancer Care. I've watched and admired them at work and then given them all the proceeds from a book. You have to do that in advance, before the book is written, putting the contract in their name. It means you work for nothing, rather than giving them instant cash.

The bit I find hard to do is responding to a knock at the door, a smile in the street with a charity box or a stab at your heart through an emotional advertisement. My wife does it without thinking, without even remembering she has done it.

I like to think I help enough charities as it is with my various subscriptions to arts and environmental societies whose meetings I never go to, whose officials I do not want to meet, or whose little magazines I buy even though their contents are totally amateur and pathetic. I have just, in fact, made what I consider my biggest single charitable contribution of the year. I paid £950 for my new season ticket for Tottenham Hotspur, yet I won't be back in London until October. It's best to see Spurs as a charity, a way of helping the poor and pathetic and wretched, or you just wouldn't do it.

"No man but a blockhead ever wrote,
except for money."
– Samuel Johnson

STAND BY YOUR BEDS — HERE ARE MY TOP TIPS FOR INVESTORS

— £ —

I am often asked the same question, being an expert, a vastly experienced man of the world. No, it's not about my teeth or whether I colour my hair. It's about finances.

"Where shall I put my money, Hunt?"

"On the counter," I say. "And buy me a drink."

"Don't be silly," they reply. "Where should I invest it, for the long term, in these troubled times, as shares are rubbish and interest rates a nonsense? With your great wisdom, what do you suggest, what worked out right for you?"

"Right." I say, "Stand by your beds. Here are my five top tips."

- A pension is the key thing. Every expert will tell you that, so the sooner you start the better. Don't worry about present trends, you won't regret it. I will always pride myself on my foresight in putting everything into, er, Equitable Life. Hold on, I'll start again.

- Stamps are brilliant. No, they really are. Look at all the articles about huge price rises — this is the time to get in. They are portable and such fun, so you can't go wrong, as long as you buy quality and get expert help, just as I did in 1979 when I invested £4,000 in a portfolio selected by Stanley Gibbons. I sold it at Sotheby's in 1999 for, don't go away, I have the details somewhere. Yes, I sold it for £1,500. Clever, huh? They don't catch me. Well, not often.

- Art, that's really the thing to invest in. If it all goes wrong, you have something nice to hang on your wall, to enjoy forever. I bought a Lowry drawing in Carlisle 20 years ago for £100, a huge amount, I thought, for a couple of matchstick men done in pencil. But I've had fun saying to guests, no Flora didn't do it when she was four, nor did the tortoise run over it. It's an original Lowry, oh yes.

  Last week I went into the Castlegate Gallery in Cockermouth as I heard they had a Lowry drawing for sale. It's a very nice one, of Maryport, much bigger than mine. I inquired about the price, which also turned out to be a great deal bigger than mine: £29,500. Cripes. I had to lie down. You thought I might be going to say I'd made a mistake. Obviously I didn't. Except I should have bought loads of them at the time. If I sell my little one now, how will I invest the money I would have made? Buy more Lowrys? You must be mad. Not at those prices.

- Beatles memorabilia. The same thing happened here. The prices are now sky high for anything decent which means I can't afford the prices. And because everyone knows or thinks they know that everything to do with the Beatles is worth a fortune, you don't see stuff on stalls any more. They put them into auctions at Sotheby's, which means that you, the buyer, have to pay an extra 17.5%. Diabolical. They won't catch me on that one.

- Football memorabilia is my present collecting passion. I've been at it now for five years, during which time the world at large has latched on to what is happening, alas. One of the areas I deliberately went into because prices were low, and most collectors were not interested, was England–Scotland football programmes. Now they've shot up and I won't pay the prices. Okay, that's a lie. I did buy three at Sotheby's in May, plus a collection of Spurs programmes. Got them for what I thought was a reasonable price. I even stomached the buyer's premium. But then, bloody hell, they demanded an extra £72 for posting—or shipment as they call it—up here to me in Lakeland. Normal first class post, which was all I required, would have been about £2. So that's it. I'm never buying at auction again, unless I'm in London.

But there is another problem. I know this wealthy collector who has hired three people to look out for football stuff, both here and in Europe. No wonder prices have risen. And that's what happens at times like this, when normal, conventional places for your money are lousy investments. People with real money rush into collecting. The best time to collect is when stocks and shares are high, so nobody writes about alternative investments. Until then, perhaps the best thing to do, since you are standing by your bed, is to keep any spare money under it.

More well-knowns who went bankrupt:

- Former Tory MP and junior minister Neil Hamilton, bankrupt in 2001
- Former Tory MP Jonathan Aitken, bankrupt in 1999
- Actor Bill Roache — Ken Barlow in *Coronation Street* — bankrupt in 1999
- Former Newcastle and Arsenal footballer Malcolm MacDonald, bankrupt in 1992
- Late comedian Rod Hull, bankrupt in 1994

A BOUQUET FOR THE MONEY MEN

— £ —

I will not have a word said against anyone in financial services. They are all wonderful people, salt of the earth, hard-working, honest, caring, kind to a fault. Don't scoff, I mean it.

I was first aware of their wonderfulness about 20 years ago when I was thinking of changing my account from the Midland Bank in London's King's Cross. I banked there for historical reasons, because it was on my way to work in Gray's Inn Road. But when I started working from home, it became very awkward, especially trying to find a parking meter. Someone at the bank asked me not to leave.

"If you get done for parking, we'll pay the fine," he said.

Now wasn't that lovely? So thoughtful. Then a new manager arrived and denied such a promise had ever been made, so I left. But I'll always treasure that offer. People in banks can be human. Last year I got a letter from the Trafalgar Square branch of Bristol & West where I have some money. I can't remember how I came to have it there, as I've never been there in my life. The letter said the branch had been redesigned to create a relaxed atmosphere.

"Sit back and take it easy in a comfortable armchair with a cup of tea or coffee and chat with our friendly staff," it said.

I pinned the letter on my wall, just to show moaners—the sort who rubbish and mock banks and building societies. And also to remind myself to pop in for a free cuppa and a chat. They didn't say about what, so my idea was to go in and chat for a few hours about football. A month later I got another letter. Due to flooding at the bank, coffee was off. All the same, I was very touched.

Last week friends of mine got a bunch of flowers from NatWest. It was not quite out of the blue. They have a small portfolio managed by the bank but it is always changing staff. After my friend rang up to complain, once again, about a different expert looking after the money, a bouquet arrived. Sweet.

In the post this morning there was a letter from Chase de Vere.

'Dear Mr and Mrs Davies, I'm delighted to announce that after working round the clock to negotiate a leading deal, we think we've come up with an ideal home for your money...'

How nice, said my wife, imagining them working all night on our behalf. That's just the sort of great people we have in finance these days, I replied. Some might say they should go home and get a good night's sleep, not risk falling asleep on the job, but I agree with you, pet.

Cheers for Chase de Vere.

Now if you happen to be one of those types who unfortunately have become rather cynical about such marvellous professional people, you might say that all these examples are minor, not to say piddling. Flowers and coffee and even parking fines are mere gestures that don't cost much. Let me tell you about my friend Ken. Ten years ago a well-known firm of financial advisers recommended that he leave his company pension scheme and take out a private pension with a big Scottish life insurer. He agreed to put in £10,000 a year in the belief that at 60 he would get a good lump sum, plus £28,000 a year. The money in his pot should have risen to £320,000 by now, this year, but it's only £75,000. He'd be lucky to get a pension of more than £5,000. He realised he'd made a terrible mistake and asked my advice. I do like to share my wisdom, being an expert on all money matters, and with my own piggy bank.

No chance, Ken, I said, after two seconds' thought. You won't get a penny extra out of them unless they gave you a guarantee. Well, he said, they did give me some possible figures. Not enough, I said. I'd forget it if I were you, squire. Guess what's happened. After a long legal battle, the financial advisers have now coughed up. They have added an extra £ 250,000 to his pension fund to ensure that he gets what he was promised. Ken is elated by the news, saying he feels as if he's won the lottery. So he's gone and spent £200,000 on a holiday home in the

Algarve. I've been invited to visit.

Now isn't that kind, isn't that caring? I mean the financial advisers, not just Ken. Would a politician have done that if his promises had not worked out? Would they heck. So no, I will not have a word said against our financial friends. The only problem is that Ken has now received an £8,000 bill. Not from the financial firm but from the solicitors who fought his case. Lawyers, eh. I bet they never give money back, offer anyone a free cup of coffee or a bunch of chrysanthemums. So hurrah for the lovely, kindly people in our financial services. Thank you.

"Money burns a hole in your pocket."
– dates from 1530

"Money doesn't talk — it swears."
– Bob Dylan

LIFE DOESN'T COME WITH
A 20-YEAR GUARANTEE

— £ —

One of my daughters had a birthday last week and her boyfriend gave her some clothes, possibly a frock, or some shoes or maybe a dressing gown. Anyway they fit her, that's the point. Then he took her out for dinner and the waiter appeared with a bouquet, which the boyfriend had organised.

"Isn't that lovely," said my wife.

Soppy, I call it. I've got more important things to think about, such as rising damp. We have just come back from five months in Lakeland and for some reason decided to move a couch in the kitchen. It revealed that while we'd been away, the wall behind had caught this nasty disease. It looked like some form of plague — blisters and bleeding and pockmarks. We'd had an out-break ages ago which we treated by stripping the wall to the bare brick and injecting it with chewing gum or something similar. And we got a guarantee. Now where was it? It took forever to find. The guarantee turned out to be for 20 years. At the time, I probably thought 20 years would never come. It's like a mortgage. You take it on thinking that's it, it's for life, never imagining a day when it will come to an end. It still had a few years to run, so that was good, but when I looked at the plans I saw the work had been done at another place, in another alcove. Oh no. This was going to cost a fortune.

"Do you remember when Richard, our daughter's boyfriend, took her on holiday to France?" said my wife. "Walking down this deserted beach they came across a bottle of champagne and two glasses, behind a rock. They were hidden by him; so romantic." Yes I remember, and what I remember is thinking: what is your game, son? Look, I am busy. I haven't time for twitting on about birthday presents, past or present.

I did try to give my wife a rather unusual birthday present once. I was a bus conductor in Carlisle, during a student vacation, and she got on my bus on her birthday. Being flash, I said she could have a free ride.

"Certainly not," she said. "I insist on paying. And I want my ticket."

Funny how these stupid incidents stick in your mind. Probably because I was jumped by an inspector a few stops later. If she hadn't had a ticket, one of us would have been for it.

I have given her clothes over the years, some of which did fit, but not recently — she's got enough by now. I have taken her out for meals. Sometimes I have even bought flowers. But not all three together, at the same time, I don't want to spoil her. Young men today, I think they get carried away. My dad never bought flowers in his life. Nor did he ever push a pram. Real men didn't.

I contacted the little local firm that did the original damp proofing and they gave me an estimate of £2,000. Seems enormous for a few feet of wall. So I rang a big, national firm that I used many years ago when we had loft problems. A woman on the phone said it would be £50 for a callout. I said I just wanted an estimate, not to invest in the firm. I couldn't believe it. Surely all building firms still give you free estimates, even in these hard times? So I'm sitting here wondering what to do about the house, trying not to listen to any more soppy present stories. I don't mind spending money on improvements. Well I do, but at least there's the satisfaction of knowing you've got something for your money. What I hate is splashing out just to keep it all from falling to pieces.

Do you think, my sweet, that we could manage to live with the pockmarks and bleeding plaster? I mean, damp is not infectious—it doesn't cause cholera or impetigo. And it's not dangerous. The house won't fall down, I don't think. It's not really so unattractive, if we keep the lights low. Surely we can put up with a bit of flaky plaster for the next few years, until at last we reach that wonderful state of nirvana when, whatever happens in the house, we can always say those magic words:

"It'll see us out."

Tell you what, I said, let's move the couch back. Out of sight, out of mind. So that's what I've done. Instead, I'm going to spend the money on really good Christmas presents for my dear ones. He's right, that boyfriend. Lash out on the here and now, give pleasure, reap the rewards, bugger the future. Life, after all, doesn't come with any 20-year guarantees.

"Do they use a different currency in the north?"
– Jade Goody, *Big Brother* contestant

"Instead of getting married again, I'm going to find a woman I don't like and just give her a house."
– Actor, Steven Segal

"Money can't buy you happiness but it does bring you a more pleasant form of misery."
– Spike Milligan

BETTER HALF IS ALL THAT'S LEFT
OF MY INVESTMENTS

— £ —

I've had this awfully nice letter from Equitable Life, as I'm sure a million others have. I wasn't going to mention the company again, ever, but why be petty?

'We have done our best to protect you,' the letter says, going on to suggest that, really, people like me have been very lucky, with Equitable Life looking after us so jolly well. I instantly felt such guilt, especially when the letter pointed out that, 'Basically, with-profits annuities, like yours, are now out of line by about 30%'. What a selfish pig I have been these past few years, taking money from these nice people.

However, the firm has now decided to even things up. From February 1, my annuity will be reduced by up to 20%. 'This letter gives you some warning before your next review date.' So kind, taking the trouble to tell me, well in advance. I was going to write back to one of the executives, send him a few bob, because he's made me feel so greedy. But I think he may be one of those who has recently gone, after half an hour or so sorting things out, taking with him probably a very measly redundancy package. My wife and I put a fortune into Equitable over the decades. I took it all out, as an annuity, about three years ago and have been getting roughly £2,000 a month. Enough, so I thought, to keep us going on bread and butter and Beaujolais. But from February, I will be getting £400 less a month.

I can roughly remember signing the forms, all those years ago. The two men in suits told me to ignore that with-profits bit—don't worry, all it means is we will even things up, year by year, so you will end up getting the same, or better, every year.

The same day I heard from Equitable I got a letter from Scottish Mutual. Lovely people, Scottish, of course, no nonsense. I put £25,000 into an income bond with the firm three years ago, receiving 8% interest a year, with the return on my capital dependent on the performance of the Dow Jones Euro Stoxx 50, whatever that is. The breathless prose in the accompanying leaflet said: 'Historically, the Euro Stoxx has never fallen over a three-year period since data became available.' Well, that sounded reassuring. Now I discover that it's fallen so far it's out of sight. The maturity level on December 12, when it's due, is likely to be only 50%. In other words, £12,500 is down the drain. I have been paid interest of £5,500 over the past three years, so my overall loss will be only £7,000. Lucky me, not totally wiped out.

I don't remember anyone in a suit, but Investors Direct, which wrote to me with this exciting offer, urged me to hurry, hurry, invest quickly to avoid disappointment. It never struck me at the time as gambling. I thought I was being, wait for it, here it comes: prudent. But I am lucky, I have made other provisions. And I've just been upstairs to check on my major investment. I have nailed my wife to her desk, pen in hand, and there she'll stay, working, until I let her out.

Peter Altenberg, the Austrian poet who died in 1919, had a habit of begging for money. The critic Karl Kraus remembered how Altenberg had pleaded and pleaded with him once for one hundred kronen.

"I just don't have the money," said Kraus, "So I can't give it to you."

"All right then, said Altenberg, "I'll lend it to you."

CHAPTER FIVE

Flats, peps, medicines, wines and socks

— £ —

PEPS ARE COBBLERS —
I'M OFF ON HOLIDAY

In my fantasy life I will no longer have an accountant and will no longer have to fill in tax returns. I will have a modest income that is all tax-free so I no longer have any paperwork. Ah, wouldn't that be bliss. All impossible of course. Dying is about the most reliable way of achieving such a state. Death, so they say, is the only journey you ever take for which you don't need to pack. Which is smart, clever, glib, but not quite true. You do have to pack, in the sense that it's best to make a will and leave your affairs in a reasonable state, unless of course you are a single person, owning nothing, with no family. Then you can just pop off, no probs.

Last week two very nice financial advisers from HSBC came to see me. Can't remember how they came to call. Did they knock? Did I answer some dopey advert? Financial advisers do just seem to materialise, creep up unawares, contact you at a vulnerable, empty, boring time. And before you realise it, they are here, in your life, drinking tea—two sugars for the younger suit—admiring the furniture and the books, and being ever so pleasant and human.

Now it all comes back to me. The bank did ask if I wanted any advice, spouting a list, none of which I wanted. But one of them was to do with Peps, offering to knock them into shape. I've had Peps and the like from the beginning, investing something each year, because there are tax advantages, so it does seem sensible. Then I've forgotten about them. Stuff has come in, which I ignore, forgetting how much I put in and why, especially when they've changed their names, becoming new beings I don't recognise. Behind my back, they have metamorphosed.

Each time when their statements have come in I have been mystified by the names and also by how little they were worth. Then I have shoved them into a drawer and forgotten them.

These advisers said they would analyse them all, see what was doing well and what was rubbish, and then put them into one big pot and look after them all for me. Wasn't that kind? They would move things around if they were doing poorly, and let me have one report each year, instead of this mountain of paper.

I signed the forms, as I liked the idea of getting some of my bits of paper in order. They would charge 3% as an initial fee, which on £60,000 of our joint Peps came to £1,800, then an annual fee of 1%. This, of course, is on top of the 1% or so levied by the individual funds. So the idea was to pay extra so that investments that were already losing money would perhaps lose a little less thanks to HSBC's great brains, all their fingers, all their computers. Nobody expected them actually to rise — just to do better than I would do on my own. Before they left, I asked how their portfolio had done. It was down 26% in two-and-a-half years. Hmm. Not very reassuring. After they'd gone I couldn't sleep for thinking about it. The last time I let financial advisers into the house they were from Equitable Life. Enough said.

So I've just rung them to say I'm cancelling it, the first time in about 20 years I've done that, using the seven-day cancellation period. Instead I'm going to sell all the Peps that are doing badly. They point out I will lose my tax-free advantages but bugger that. No point in having a tax advantage when there's no profit. So bang goes the first stage in my fantasy of making my life simple.

 Paul Getty, the oil-rich art collector, was asked if it was true that he was worth a billion dollars.

"I suppose so," he said. "But don't forget, a billion doesn't go as far as it used to go."

MY CHEAPSKATE TRIP TO
THE LAND OF ARGOS

— £ —

It's our elder daughter's birthday on March 6, so I suggested we buy her a TV.

"Good idea," said my wife. "Let's get a video recorder as well," and she was ringing John Lewis before I could stop her.

"What are you doing, woman?" I shrieked.

"Ordering a TV and video," she replied. "You can do it on the phone. John Lewis is always good quality and delivery is free. It's all so easy."

I grabbed the phone before she could give her Visa card number.

"Are you potty? TVs and videos are two things that have dropped in price; burglars don't even bother to nick them. And they all work, even if you've never heard of the make. So it doesn't matter where you get them. Here, I'll organise this. Leave it to me, pet."

The person from John Lewis on the other end was clearly mystified by all the shouting. I asked for the price of their cheapest video and 21-inch TV: £99 and £239.

"Thank you my good man," I said, "I'll think about it." Thinking: no chance, I bet I can get it cheaper.

I went down to the High Road and spent a whole morning going round the TV shops. You have to be there, oh yes, just in case there's a special offer, a half term, half-price deal, or something shop-soiled, last one left, hurry hurry. I went to both Dixons and Currys to check them out. I know they're owned by the same people but you never know, offers vary. Then I went to Argos, the catalogue shop. I had never been in Argos before. It's like a foreign country, with its own language, where they do things differently. What's the capital of Argos, I wondered, do they have a king or a president? So many queues and counters, all very confusing. But I found a catalogue and wrote down the details.

Then I came home and studied the prices, working out that the cheapest video was at Dixons, £64.99, while the cheapest 21-inch TV was at Argos, £99.99.

What a bargain.

"You're not going to two different shops, are you?" said my wife. "At least get them from the same place and have them delivered, make it easy for yourself."

"Delivered? They'll charge a fortune. I'll use the car, after we've been to Marks & Spencer for the weekly shop."

Carrying the video from Dixons was easy enough. Then I returned to Argos, which took forever. It was like a bingo hall, not that I've ever been in one, or a betting shop. They give you a little pen and you have to fill in a slip. You queue to pay, then queue again, waiting for your number to be called out. When the TV eventually emerged from the hinterland of Argos — they keep them far away in a distant part of the country — it was enormous, far too big and heavy for me to carry.

So I raced back to Marks, got the car and my wife with the shopping. I had to make a massive detour, as the High Road is one-way. I parked outside Argos on a double yellow line, or it might even have been a red. I told her to sit tight in the car and if a traffic warden comes, just say 'no speaka da English'.

I staggered out with the TV, knackering my knees, only to find it was too big to put inside the car.

"I'll get a taxi and take it home," said my wife.

"You will not. Do you know how much taxis cost?"

I got it in the boot but it wouldn't shut, so I went into Argos again to get some string, but I couldn't find a way to tie it. We stood there in the High Road screaming at each other. Buses were queuing up behind us, honking away, and then a traffic warden arrived and began to take the registration number of my Jaguar. Yes, my Jaguar. Five years old, second hand, but all the same a pretty posho car to be seen tied up with string while we stand outside Argos shouting. Oh, the humiliation. I just hope none of our neighbours were on the buses.

We got home in the end with my wife in despair. Will I never learn, will I never change? So she asked me.

"What do you mean? I've saved all this money. We've only spent £165. You would have paid £338."

"Yes, but you could easily afford it, have done it in minutes, and saved yourself all that stress and all that time."

She's right, of course. And, the worst thing is, I know that in a year, perhaps just a few months, I will have forgotten what the TV and video cost. I'll just remember I saved money. However much it was.

Do I need therapy?

"Dally not with women or money."
1640, G. Herbert, *Outlandish Proverbs*

A very silly piece of advice. Who is going to be bothered obeying that in 2005? And I bet they mostly ignored it in 1640. Fortunately we have a lot more to dally with in life today. Football, that's one for a start. Television, the internet, iPods, smokey bacon crisps. Women and money have a lot of competition for dalliers today.

SPURS SEASON TICKET WAS
A REAL OWN GOAL

— £ —

Careful and prudent, that's how I see myself, counting the pennies so the pounds can count themselves. It's a good job I do. You wouldn't believe how people in this house still leave coins lying around — on the hall shelf, on the Welsh dresser, emptying their pockets of pennies when they go out or come in.

While being careful and prudent, I can also be completely wasteful, not caring what things cost. For example, a few weeks ago I didn't go to Spurs, I just couldn't face it. Going to an evening match means not being able to have a proper drink with my evening meal. I would lose four hours and be in bed late. And it was only against Fulham. So, at the last moment, I decided to watch it on television.

"What?" said my wife. "You are not going? The man who hates waste? Wait until I tell the children."

I have a Spurs season ticket that cost £954, so I was throwing away the equivalent of £50. Oh, the agonies of indecision I went through all day, until it was too late to give the ticket to someone else. In the end, my seat lay empty, a symbol of my wild, spendthrift nature.

"You'll come to want," said my wife. "Which reminds me. When are you taking back that briefcase?"

She bought it for me two Christmases ago, real leather, very posh. It cost about £80 and she gave me the receipt so I could change it. I have never used it or been able to get up the energy to go to Oxford Street. I try to blank it from my mind, as I know it means I have deliberately wasted £80.

Two years ago, I spent a day checking out computers in Tottenham Court Road, thinking I must get to grips with the modern world. A laptop would be so handy when I'm travelling or in the Lake District, so I bought one for £800. After a week, I hated it. My fingers were too big for the keyboard, so I gave it to our younger daughter, Flora. It hasn't been wasted, she's got it on permanent loan. That eases my conscience, though I know I was stupid, throwing money around.

Even dafter, I've gone and done it again. On Boxing Day I went off to the sales at PC World and bought a proper computer at the bargain price of £420. Something called an 'E-machine'. I did check the keyboard carefully and it's excellent, no problems there, but I loathe the monster tower that comes with all computers. It's so ugly and it hums all the time. And I find the mouse thing very annoying. The computer does have lots of marvellous facilities, none of which I want. I worked out the email system, but then people started sending me emails back. Most were boring, so I stopped. I looked up stuff on the internet but it was either rubbish or out of date. Worst of all, it took me so long to write on it. Even writing a simple article took ages.

So I am now back on my ancient Amstrad PCW9512 on which I have written 2m words in the past 10 years, what with books and stuff. I love it dearly. It does everything I want, quickly, easily, no fuss. Yes, I have to fax copy or hand in a book manuscript on paper but hard cheese. They've coped with that for decades. I know, I know, don't tell me. I can't go on like this forever, using out-of-date technology. Everyone and his tortoise has a computer today. Even people who never write more than one page a year have their gleaming computer sitting there proudly. Fifty years ago, households had to have a cocktail cabinet. My parents had one, cheap shiny wood with glass sliding doors which they kept proudly in the parlour, yet they never drank a cocktail in their lives.

Computers are the modern equivalent of cocktail cabinets. Mine is now shoved in a corner, staring at me. It's £452 down the drain, because I bought a printer as well. All my children have their own computers, so I can't even lend it out. My wife only ever uses a fountain pen. I thought about putting it in the loft but now I plan to keep it as a conversation piece. See that thing over there, cost a fortune, but I never use it. That's the sort of person I am. Let nobody say I am mean with money.

"Money begets money."
First spotted in a book of proverbs in 1572.
Sometimes reads as "Money breeds money."
Just as spot on, really.

AN ISA FROM HALIFAX? JUST RING BOMBAY, OR GLASGOW — OR MARS

— £ —

What I really want in life is a guaranteed return. I don't mean returning whence we came—that's certain, although the length of the wait is not guaranteed. No, I want to know where I am with my money and what sort of returns I can expect, tax-free, if possible. So when I saw an advert for a mini cash Isa from Halifax, guaranteeing 4.35% tax-free over five years, I thought that sounds good, though what the hell is mini cash? Do you have to pay it in halfpennies or dolls' currency?

I've always put £7,000 in a full Isa—I'm not sure if 'full' is the correct term—which seemed to be what you did, what the government wanted us to do. Every year the newspapers are crammed with alluring ads for such Isas and leaflets drop through the letterbox on the hour. I suspect you hear so much about them because financial advisers get a good cut for selling them.

I rang the number in the Halifax advert and was put through to a voice in Milton Keynes, or Glasgow, or Bombay, or Mars. I asked for an application form. Not possible, they said. You have to go in to a branch. No problem, I said. Send me the train fare for Glasgow or Bombay, and I'll be right round.

"Your local branch," said a world-weary voice. "Where do you live?"

I told them and there was a long pause while they located the nearest branch. I knew the street but I was unaware it had a Halifax. They said they could book an appointment for me. How kind. For two of us, actually, as I was sure my dear wife would want to put her £3,000 of halfpennies in a mini cash Isa. I rushed upstairs to my wife's room to check she could make the date, five days ahead.

"Get out," she said. "I'm working."

I said it was urgent, mini cash Isa, 4.35% tax-free, best rate in the universe, including Mars.

"What's a mini cash Isa?" she asked. "Some sort of car?"

"Look, I haven't time to explain things, can you make Tuesday at 3pm, yes or no?"

It was no. I had to rush up and down several times, liasing with Bombay, until we eventually agreed a date. I was told to bring means of identification. Later that day, I realised I was already a member of the Halifax. One of the many stupid investments I had with

Equitable Life metamorphosed into something with Halifax Financial Services. Surely they are the same out-fit?

I got the phone book out to look for the number of the Halifax branch where we had our appointment, to see if we still needed identification—and couldn't find it. About 80 Halifax branches are listed, all with an 0845 number, which of course means Bombay, an hour of waiting and crap music. Bloody hell. The Halifax is as bad as my bank, HSBC. They keep their branch phone numbers secret, as if they're MI5.

We went on the bus as we had so much to carry: our passports, utility bills, bank statements, birth certificates, driving licences, my patrol leader's badge from the Boy Scouts, and her award for public speaking from Carlisle and County High School for Girls. I was doing them the favour, giving them our money to play with, for a measly 4.35%, yet they were making it so awfully hard. But we did it. We now have our mini cash Isas. Even more exciting, I managed to get the phone number of the Kentish Town branch of the Halifax. I'm sworn to secrecy but I'm willing to swap, if you have David Beckham's or Tony Blair's private number.

The biggest football spenders are the Scottish, while those in the North East, Yorkshire and London spend the least.

Region	Supporters' average spend
Scotland	£332
East Anglia	£295
South East	£295
South West	£238
Wales	£238
North West	£209
Midlands	£205
London	£191
North East	£191
Yorkshire	£191

MY CHILD FEELS ROBBED AND I'M THE PRIME SUSPECT

— £ —

Only one of my offspring has any passing interest in money. I blame their mother. I've always been on at them not to leave anything in their current accounts; to look for the best deal; why let other people take advantage of your savings; look after the pennies; and so on. Boring, boring, they usually say, before I've even got to the end of my sanctimonious spiel.

But one of them, two years ago, told me proudly about seeing a financial adviser. I was expected to cheer, but I didn't, believing as I do that advisers are to be listened to and then ignored. But I smiled, paternally, and said, 'Not a bad idea, you'll learn something'. It then turned out to be an adviser provided by Barclays Bank. Oh help, I thought. All they can recommend are their own products but I nodded and said, 'Well, it's a start'. More than a start, so it transpired. The life savings and birthday presents involved, which came to the vast sum of £7,000, had been put into a Barclays unit-trust Isa. Barclays' advice was that this was a safe, tax-efficient investment. Last week, it was worth £5,500 and still falling. And it's all my fault. Oh yes it is. I've got the blame. But for me twitting on, the money would have been left in a bank account and would be a good few hundred pounds in profit by now.

We've all been caught, of course. I have Peps, Isas and Tessas going back ages, and they're all rubbish. Over the past 30 years or so, since I first had some money left over at the end of the month, this is the worst time I can remember. Almost always in the past I put the money into building society bonds with modest returns—but returns there were, not losses. Then over the years I too got seduced by all these things with no tax to pay on any profits—hurry, hurry. But we were all conned. It's hard to see any tax advantages when there are no profits. Yes, we all know the basic reason. Stuff tied up in the stock market, which means almost everything, has dropped about 20% in two years. So it goes. I can wait and look forward to better days, better rates, and also look back to all the solid sensible investments with sensible names I made in ye olden days that never backfired.

But the young generation, starting now, are finding that investing money is a risky business, even when they do the apparently sensible thing and invest with a famous name like Barclays. They try awfully hard to understand all the fancy terms and confusing rules but end up feeling cheated, wishing they'd kept their money under their beds or, best of all, spent it on themselves.

"Do you realise, Dad, that my £1,500 that has been lost because of you could have bought a brilliant round-the-world holiday? By the way, Dad, where has it gone? How can it just disappear, Hunt? Who's got my £1,500? You're supposed to be clever with money. Give me names and addresses, I've got some friends who could sort them."

Er, it doesn't quite work that way, dear children. Money, in a sense, is an abstract concept. Nobody has gone off with it, because the value is, er, notional. Actually, good question, let Daddy think about it for a moment. But they were off to the pub, to spend, spend, spend.

The government should be alarmed that this genera-tion could be put off saving money for life, preferring to spend every spare penny on drink, clothes, clubs, the gym, holidays, good times. And I'm alarmed that I couldn't answer my children's question. I know when you sell unit trusts at a profit, it's because somebody is prepared to pay that price for them. But when they drop by 20%, where does the money go? Who's got it? I think I need to talk to a financial adviser.

Ben Hecht, the American playwright, made a lot of money out of the Florida property boom of the 1920s. He never really believed it would last, but during the good times, he appeared to grow plumper and plumper, as if enjoying himself on his windfalls. In reality he was carrying rolls of banknotes on his body, not trusting them to a bank. When a crash came, he was one of the few to escape with all his money intact.

AN ISA TOO FAR FOR THE TAXMAN

— £ —

We've received a letter from the Inland Revenue saying we have broken the rules. It's actually to my wife, she's the one who is supposed to have transgressed — which of course she hasn't, being a model of all the virtues.

I handle money matters in our house, so none of it is her fault. Not only have I done wrong, I've got her into trouble as well. Oh no. Will she go to jail? If she does, who will bring me tea in bed in the morning? And turn on the radio for me? This is all far more serious than I thought.

Then I'll get a talking to from my accountant. For about four years now his firm has been trying to get me to take out insurance cover in the event of an Inland Revenue investigation. He has told me that they can do a random inquiry at any time, which could be very expensive. The firm has arranged its own scheme. All I have to do is pay the premium each year. I've refused — on principle. I don't agree with insurance. My principle is based on stupidity but I've stuck to it for more than 30 years now, avoiding insurance whenever I can, such as life or health insurance. Never had either. And I'm still here, sort of.

I told my accountant that my affairs were in order. I don't fear random investigation. Anyway, if it happens, I bet I'll have most of the paperwork to do, scratching around in the garage for old bills and invoices that the rats have not yet eaten. So I'll take my chances, thank you very much.

This particular Inland Revenue letter, once I read it all properly, was to do with Isas. Apparently in 2001, my wife took out two, which is not allowed—a mini cash one with Bristol and West and a maxi with NDF. I couldn't remember taking out either and I've no idea what NDF stands for. Nearly Dead Fund? No Damn Fun?

I scrabbled around and eventually found details of both. Then it came back to me. I had a bond with Bristol & West that matured in 2001. One of the bank's advisers came to see me and suggested I invest the money in several brilliant products. All of them, surprisingly, turned out to be with Bristol and West. They included a mini Isa. So I signed the form , forgetting I already had one.

I rang the Inland Revenue person who had written to us and apologised profusely, all my fault, a silly mistake, though the Inland Revenue letter contained a small mistake as well. The number it gave for one Isa was incorrect. It belonged to someone else. But it was true that my wife had two Isas. What do we do now? How serious is it? Hanging or what? My Inland Revenue friend sounded very laid back. He said that 30,000 people had done the same thing. All we had to do was get rid of the mini cash Isa or convert part of the maxi Isa to another sort of mini Isa, which sounded very complicated and I didn't quite understand it.

I never realised that you can, in fact, have two mini Isas, if they are different types, but not a maxi and a mini. Gawd, don't they make life complicated. But I suppose it does keep tax officers off the streets and accountants in Mercedes.

I've decided the simplest thing is to sell off the maxi Isa. In looking into the details of both investments, which I had forgotten we ever had, I discovered something else I should have been aware of if I am the self-appointed money brains in this house — they are both rubbish. I have lost, not gained by this silly mistake. And it would probably have got worse.

So thank you, Inland Revenue, for pointing it out. You've helped a lot.

"Words are but sands, money buys lands."
1659, *Howell's English Proverbs*

DAY MY WIFE HIT ME WITH A £359 COVER CHARGE

— £ —

I was driving into Cockermouth for my twice-weekly swim when my wife told me the news. What a shock. I managed to avoid some stray Herdwick sheep in the road and drove into a field to calm down. We have this old armchair in our bedroom, which we bought for £10 some 15 years ago at Mitchells auction rooms. It's perfectly okay, if a bit battered and frayed, but aren't we all. Nobody uses it for sitting on. I just chuck clothes on it.

My wife told me she had replied to an advert in *The Sunday Times Magazine* and allowed a 'professionally trained home consultant' into our house. She had also agreed that a loose cover should be made for the chair, at a cost of £179. Bloody hell, I said, swerving to avoid the sheep. And then, totally wilfully, she took the consultant downstairs where we have an old Chesterfield-type sofa. This, too, is to be recovered for — I can't believe I'm writing this — £359! That is my first exclamation marks in 40 years as a journalist. Has the world and my wife gone mad?

"Oh that's cheap," she said.

Joan, our neighbour, guessed the price would be double that, so my wife alleges. And Annabell, my own sister, thought it was a bargain.

"I don't want you talking to either of those women again," I ordered.

"It's being done by Plumbs Covers," she said. "They're very good."

I'd never heard of Plumbs Covers until, by chance last January, we met Mr and Mrs Plumb on holiday.

"No wonder they can afford expensive hols," I said.

"So can we," said my wife.

Refurbishment, of any sort, is what I most hate spending money on. Buying new things, which will give extra value and extra enjoyment, such as a conservatory or summer house, I can easily do. Well, not easily, but I manage it. But spending fortunes on stuff you already have to make it look, well, just the same, is money down the old drain.

When we arrived here in May, for our six-month stay in Lakeland, we found that our 15-year-old Indesit dishwasher had packed up. The call-out charge, just to look at it, was going to be £65, plus at least another £40 for the new part. But when they heard it was more than nine years old, they wouldn't even come out. The modern world doesn't want you to have things repaired, only to buy new machinery. A new Indesit costs only £208, just twice the price of having the old one repaired, so I managed to sign the cheque, with my eyes closed, teeth gritted.

The dishwasher was broken but the sofa is working. You can still sit on it. Who cares about frayed edges? If you are so passionate about re-covering it, why not do it yourself, pet? Didn't I give you a sewing machine in 1964? I did, and she made all our curtains and loose covers herself. Very badly, and hated it. She's certainly not doing that again. One of our daughters got the sewing machine and promptly sold it. Nobody does their own sewing today. So how clever of the Plumbs, who started with a market stall and now have a multi-million-pound business, sewing for other people.

But answer me this, woman. If we fall on hard times and have to sell the recovered sofa, how much will we get? I bet Mr and Mrs Plumb wouldn't give you a tenner for it, nor any of their hordes of home consultants. It certainly won't fetch £359. Oh no, the price has passed my lips again. I vowed to wipe it from my mind, pretend it hasn't happened.

That's the only way to deal with such nasty things in life. I've decided I don't want to be told any more about so-called necessary refurbishments. You don't have to lie to me. Just keep it as your little secret.

 "Money comes from him likes drops of his blood."
Quoted in a collection of English proverbs
edited by J. Ray, 1678.

MY BOATHOUSE DREAM

— £ —

I've just been to look at a boathouse. Inside, it's basically water, where you can keep a little boat, hence the name boathouse. I think I've made that clear enough. The price is £135,000. Gulp.

Garages in London can go for that amount, so we in Cumbria have been led to believe, but of course they're all daft in London. Here we're usually much more sensible, though the boathouse would appear to be a reasonable price, judging by the level of interest.

It's on Ullswater, perhaps the loveliest of the lakes. I fell in love with its situation straightaway. What fun it would be to own it, playing at Swallows and Amazons. I can just see myself messing around in a boat with my London granddaughters, Ruby and Amelia, even though they are only three and four and probably don't know what a boat is; Tufnell Park doesn't have many. Upstairs, the loft part has been converted into a sort of little attic flat. Oh very nice. There's only one draw-back — the Lake District National Park Authority, the rotters, say it can't be slept in overnight. All the same, I came home raving about it to my wife.

I wished I'd had my camera ready to capture her look

of incredulity. You what? This is the man who moans when anyone dares to use a first class stamp and who all week has complained about phone calls to his sister. She's been in hospital in High Wycombe, Buckinghamshire. It was just for tests and everything's okay now. She had a bedside phone, which so many hospitals now provide — jolly useful, I thought, until I heard a voice announce the price would be 99p a minute. Or perhaps it was 59p. I hung up at once. Bloody hell.

And yet you are seriously considering a stupid boat-house? The sun must have warped your brain. What's the point of a house you can't sleep in? Ah, I said, it depends on the definition of sleep. I could stay awake all night or sleep standing up. I'm sure folks bend the rules all the time. Anyway, the Lake District planning board doesn't have sleep inspectors. They're too busy checking you haven't put a window in your toilet or used the wrong slates.

It also means, she pointed out, that there will be no income. You can't rent it as a holiday home. So it's a total waste of money. I never thought of that but then I'm a romantic, deep down, not a penny pinching moany minny as some in this house allege. What is the point of petty worries about interest rates, mortgages and the Equitable Life nonsense if we can't also have our dreams? Let the spirit soar, aim for loftier things, though that loft bit, now I think about it, was a bit low. You haven't got a boat either, she said. In fact, you told me you hated sailing.

I used to have a dinghy on Derwent Water but I never got the hang of the winds or sails. When trying to moor, I found the easiest way was to crash into an island. I once told Jake, our son, to jump into the water quickly and pull us onto the shore, not realising the water was 10ft deep. He disappeared.

The agent who showed me round the boathouse was Kyle Blue of PFK in Penrith. He said boathouses rarely came onto the market, hence all the interest. And it did have battery-powered electricity, water from a well and a chemical toilet. After I'd looked round, I had a brilliant swim from the boathouse. Even if I didn't have a boat, Ruby and Amelia would still love it. I can just see them now, splashing around, having picnics. You are contemplating paying £135,000 for a picnic spot? You are really going mad.

Don't worry, pet, I'm just winding you up. I agree, it would be a stupid thing to do. On the other hand, Mr Blue tells me that later in the year another boathouse may come up for sale that can legally be used to sleep in. Now that would be much more useful and a better investment, as it could be rented out. Naturally, it's likely to cost a lot more, such as £250,000. What do you think, my sweet?

If you promise to stick to second class stamps for the rest of your life and we don't make any more phone calls, we might just manage it. I hate these people obsessed by the price of things. We all need our fantasies.

"I rob banks because that's where the money is."
Bank robber, Willie Sutton

"My formula for success is rise early,
work late and strike oil."
John Paul Getty

THE BEST CURE IS THE ONE
THAT COSTS THE LEAST

— £ —

I've got arthritis. Who hasn't over the age of 60? But this isn't about arthritis, just the effects of having arthritis. One of which was something weird I learned last week. I went to have a chest X-ray at Workington Infirmary and the radiographer had to do it twice because the first time two dark shadows showed up. She put some tape and wire over my nipples and this time it was okay.

What's going on? She explained that women's nipples don't show up on an X-ray but men's do, as they get a build-up of calcium with age. Back to money. Since I developed arthritis some 10 years ago, everyone and his dog has offered advice.

"Oh, what you want to do is get some of this oil of evening vinegar, or a bottle of cats' poo pills, or cod liver chewing gummy—auntie used it, did her so much good. Yes, she is dead, but she swore by it."

So I went to the chemist to look for the potions in question but when I saw the prices I walked straight out again.

One Christmas about five years ago, my wife, bless her, bought me some stuff an old dear had recommended. It's called cat's claw, or una de gato. On the label it says it's 'Found in the rich tropical region of Brazil's rainforest'. Well, where else do you get rainforests if not the tropics—in the Arctic? She'd paid £8 for a bottle of 90 capsules. They must have seen you coming. It would be like swallowing pound notes. And do me as much good. I refused to take any. I have read that Brazil's rainforests will disappear with global warming, so the price of una de gato will rocket and I stand to make a fortune.

Over the years, I have occasionally tried various homeopathic medicines and supplements, either when they've been free, so the price hasn't stuck in my throat, or they were on special offer. I once bought an industrial-sized bottle of cod-liver oil from a dodgy-looking chemist in Archway, north London, for only £2.99— probably because it was really sump oil. I forced down a teaspoonful a day for about six months. It tasted vile but

I was saving money. Pills that are nicer to take are at least four times more expensive.

The price of all this health food nonsense seems to have doubled in the five years since my wife bought me that cat's thingy. I looked at a health shop's catalogue the other day and some tablets called ginkgo biloba, whatever they are, had been priced at £14.49. How can people afford it? They must be really sick.

But the biggest shock came last week. My GP in Cumbria has recommended something called glucosamine, a naturally occurring thingy that improves the mobility of your joints, allegedly. Oh, it's very fashionable, you see it advertised everywhere. The fact that my GP, a real doctor, was recommending it, made me less cynical. The cost of the 60 tablets, so it says on the packet, is £19.99. So that's the end of them.

My view on organic food has always been very simple. When I see the word 'organic', I substitute the word pricey. When I see the words homeopathic, I immediately see 'bloody pricey'. And yet health foods, natural remedies, herbal pills, dietary supplements and all the rest of them sell in trillions. I have to think that plenty of people believe they do some good — and not just to the manufacturers. But why are so-called natural medicines so expensive if they are, well, natural? Another thing I've noticed is that the more people pay for them, the more determined they are for you to try them. Is this to make you complicit in their own foolishness?

"But they've helped me," they cry. "Surely your health matters more than money?"

That's what old crones insist, the ones still alive and stuffing their faces with high-grade zinc, low-level fibre, dawn-kissed muck, free-range leprechaun milk.

"You can't be so mean as to deprive yourself of natural goodness, with no added nasty chemicals? You are just stupidly prejudiced."

No, I simply prefer nasty old chemical prescription drugs, as scientifically tested on humans and other animals. And once you are over 60, they are free, hurrah hurrah.

I admit this is an added bonus.

Rossini, the Italian composer, when old and famous, still did not consider himself financially secure. When he heard that a group of admirers had raised £20,000 for a statue for him, he asked them not to bother.

"Give me the money," he said. "And I'll stand on the pedestal myself."

PUT YOUR MONEY IN
NNNNNRRRRRR...

— £ —

I was driving through Camden Town last week, as we're back from Lakeland for the winter, when I saw a big glass building I'd never noticed before. On the side were some huge but rather faint letters, which seemed to be fading away. I nearly crashed trying to read them but managed to make out the word Abbe.

Then I saw there was a final letter, a Y, which appeared to be slipping. I remembered: the Abbey National has spent £11.5m to turn itself into dynamic new Abbey.

I have a Pep with the bank, somewhere, among the Peps I'm trying to forget, or it might be a with-profits bond. Either way, I'm a customer of Abbey National. The evidence is deep in a drawer, hidden away, because I don't want to be confronted by my own foolishness. But I'll continue to call it Abbey National until I get the energy to clear out the junk in the drawer.

Names do matter. I'll never forgive Midland Bank for turning into HSBC—what a mouthful, what a non-sense. If it happened today, I certainly wouldn't let them have the pleasure of my money. I remember when Egg came out. The rates looked quite good, so I got the gen. Then I decided I couldn't possibly invest money in a firm with such a silly name. By the same milk token, I have avoided Smile, Orange and Giraffe. Something called ING Direct is currently advertising like mad but how can I invest in something with half a word missing?

Sometimes, of course, you can't help it. They creep up behind your back and change their names from something clear and sensible to something bizarre, ugly or just meaningless. In my portfolio, which is how I grandly describe that bottom drawer, I have stuff from Aegon, CGNU, AIG and Legg Mason. I swear I never invested with them, not knowingly, not with such daft initials and potty names. I saw a reference in a newspaper the other day to some company called MMO2. I thought, hello, someone's hand has slipped on the computer keyboard and produced gibberish. Then I realised it was a real company, formerly something to do with BT. I could even be a customer, as my mobile phone was originally BT Cellnet. I haven't used it for two years, so I can't actually check.

There's also an even newer mobile company called 3. God, that must be confusing. It's so minimalist it disappears in the middle of a sentence. I wonder how they list it alphabetically?

The financial world loves new images, arty symbols and impressive-sounding words, even when nobody else understands what the hell they are on about. Perhaps it's to disguise the lack of content. I'm always amused by the use of their word 'product', as if the financial services industry has ever produced anything worthwhile.

A good solid sensible name has always appealed to me, which is why I still have so much money with Northern Rock. Great name, don't you think? Straightforward, nothing fancy, a name you know where you are with, each word redolent of strength and reliability. Not, of course, that any modern designer would think so, not when he or she has been given £11.5m to muck around with it and come up with something truly original and revolutionary, such as nnnnnnnnnrrrrrrrrrr. I quite like that, now I look at it on the line. Neat, huh, the way the n turns into an r. If they use it, I could be rich.

Anything beginning with 'Scottish' attracts me. We all know Scots created so many of our famous financial institutions. And I do like to hear a Scottish voice when I ring up to ask how my money is getting on. There is less chance of that today when the phones are in India and the world head office is a basement in Camden Town. There's one name I've always loved. Right from the beginning, I was so impressed by its imposing name, its royal-looking coat of arms and the fact that it was founded in 1762. I suspect that many millions, like me, became members because its name and image looked so trustworthy and solid. Now what was it called? Oh yes, Equitable Life Assurance Company. What am I saying? I take everything back. Get me out of here.

"No one would remember the Good Samaritan if he'd
only had good intentions. He had money as well."
– Margaret Thatcher

"If you want to know what God thinks of money,
just look at the people he gave it to."
– Dorothy Parker

KING OF THE JUMBLE

— £ —

Last week my son told me about an offer in a wine
shop — two bottles of Chablis for £15. He added that the
wine was very good quality. My first reaction was: what
have I bred? How come a son of mine who must be half
my age, with not a huge amount of money, plus a wife
and a four-year-old child, has noticed the price of expensive wine like Chablis?

Over the decades, my eyes have been programmed to
take in wine that has a £3 price tag, preferably £2 or £4
at a pinch. I am such an expert that I can scan shelves 100
yards away. The existence of any wine over £5 a bottle

never even registers. We have two daughters and the younger one has just had some work done in her kitchen. Not only did she get a craftsman to fix her tiles, she got another to come and do the grouting, putting on some special solution to keep it white and pristine. In our kitchen, I put on the tiles and the grout, using a knife and fork. The tiles don't fit, and of course the grout has gone grey and yucky. But the point is the work cost me nothing.

Our elder daughter is more like me: she reuses stuff, has a nose for bargains, loves jumbles. I don't think our son or younger daughter has even been to a jumble sale, nor has my wife. The elder daughter also haunts charity shops, which I think are one of the greatest inventions of my lifetime. Forget computers, mobile phones and games consoles; my life would be impoverished without charity shops. It's one of the joys of landing in a strange town, being able to head for the high street, knowing there will be at least three charity shops. They will be new to me, but oh so familiar. The smell of old clothes for a start. Hmm - breathe it in. Don't you just love it? Then there will be two women of a certain age, one a bit posh and bossy, the other dozy, wandering round in a dream.

I don't actually buy a lot these days but I like the hunt. I would have been distraught if all three of my children had mimicked my wife's disdain of such places. It is so nice to share this pleasure with one of them. I have trained her to look for things like pre-war football books. I have told her to buy them at any price, in any condition. It's good to know I have an emissary out there, working on my behalf. Like me, she is also unable to pass a skip without looking inside. The others walk by, unaware, unseeing, uninterested. What pleasures they miss in life. Do all families divide like this?

Okay, a lot of the stuff I have rescued from skips has gone back the next day, but that's not the point. As in life, it's the journey not the arrival that is the best fun. There was once a skip outside the house opposite and naturally I was having a poke around. A couple were passing on our side of the street and my wife overheard them talking.

"See that bloke over there looking in that skip," said the man to the woman. "You wouldn't believe he was a millionaire."

This is now a family legend, retold to embarrass me. But I am beyond embarrassment. How can I be ashamed when it's in my genes?

CHAPTER SIX

VAT, death, fines, regrets, I've had a few freebies

— £ —

MY SOCKS ARE IN SHREDS, IT MUST BE TIME FOR A HOLIDAY

We always wait until January to take our summer hols, when Michael Winner has got back and it's safe to walk the beaches. We'll be at Cobblers Cove once again, before moving to a rented beach cottage in Bequia. Then we'll end up at a posh place in Antigua called Carlisle Bay. As I sit here, all packed, what's really exciting me is the thought of the free socks. I have just looked in my sock drawer and last year's are in shreds, like balls of woollen spaghetti.

I do wish BA would spend a bit more on its Club Class socks. They are rather lumpen and totally shapeless, although this means they suit me fine. Have you seen my feet? They are also lumpen and shapeless but then I have got arthritis. I'm also looking forward to the bottles of shampoo in the hotel bathrooms, though I don't expect any in the rented cottage in Bequia. I'll have to pinch, I mean save, more from the hotels. Those little shampoo bottles are perfect after a swim at London's Kentish Town baths. I can make one last for months. I'll also be stocking up on note pads, the ones by our hotel bedside. And the little hotel pencils. You never know when they will come in handy.

You might think this is all silly, paying a fortune to go Club Class and stay in posh hotels, then bringing back shampoo and used airline socks. But come on, they're free. I get pleasure out of their freeness.

I always pick up those free postcards you now see in restaurants, advertising something or other. I write thank-you letters on them or notes to my children. I know it makes them smile or sneer: typical Hunter, using free postcards. See if I care. I've got no shame. Hotel note pads are particularly useful, as I can add them to my collection of headed stationery — not just from hotels, but famous places I have been, such as the White House and 10 Downing Street. They are just empty, unused stationary; they must not be written on — that's a different collection. I call it 'My Life in Notepaper'. It includes stationery from places I have worked, the oldest being a sheet of 1960 Sunday Times notepaper.

Some of the places are long gone, such as the Manchester Evening Chronicle and Punch. Headed stationery, over the years, reveals changes in ownership, location, typography and design, as well as the arrival of faxes and emails. Oh, fascinating stuff.

But this could be my last foreign holiday. I realised only yesterday that I had no travel insurance. I rang Norwich Union and was quoted £68 for my wife, but £205 for me, because I am over 65. Bloody hell! That's ageist. On a really cheapo holiday, it must mean that some 65-year-olds are paying more for their insurance than their flights and accommodation.

I have cut out endless articles from newspapers, comparing insurance prices. They are jolly helpful but of course I couldn't find them when I needed them. They are in a drawer somewhere, yellow and fading. They go back years, so they are probably well out of date, the deals and phone numbers changed. I also cut out the weekly savings tables. I have them going back decades, so they are now totally useless. Why do I bother?

I then rang Barclaycard, which took forever. How I hate all the boring options they give you. I have a Gold Visa card that includes travel insurance, I think, or have I imagined it? Am I covered? I was eventually able to ask a human voice.

"The answer is grim," a male voice replied.

What he meant was the policy covered loss of limb or death, not medical care or other stuff. He advised proper, comprehensive insurance, which meant another department and more hanging on. I was quoted £224 for the two of us together, which was an improvement. I thought of trying elsewhere as I'm sure I could get it lower still, but it could mean days hanging on and I'd miss the plane. So I took it with much heart-searching. Those free socks are becoming more expensive every year.

John D. Rockefeller, the American oil baron and philanthropist, heard that his family had ordered an electric car as a surprise birthday present for him so he could get around his large estate more easily.

"If it's all the same to you," he told his family. "I'd rather have the money."

VAT IS THE PROBLEM

— £ —

I was having lunch with a friend called Ray. People say married blokes don't have real friends; they tend to cut off such contacts. Girls, however, keep in touch with heart-to-heart chums all their lives. At least that's the supposed norm. But I have six male friends whom I lunch with every year, from Cumbria to the House of Lords.

I usually meet Ray at the Groucho Club. We don't go in for any of that boring girl chat. We discuss manly things like football and the state of our health — which can take ages — and we rubbish our enemies, especially the ones no longer in work, ha ha.

We also talk about something that women never discuss together: money. Over lunch Ray mentioned Vat, a nasty three-letter word I try not to use. He told me that he was paying 12% Vat. Are you raving Ray? Get a grip, you ignorant Scouser, you were always useless with money. Didn't they teach you nuffink at the LSE? Vat is 17.5%, do concentrate. Then the conversation moved on.

I've been registered for Vat since it began and hate all the faffing around and paperwork that it creates for millions of self-employed people like me. When it started, they used to send a Vat man once a year to look at my books, here in my so-called workplace. It meant the accountant I used had to send a bloke here with my books so we could all sit and stare at them. At least they've stopped those stupid visits but I still pay a book-keeper £150 a quarter to fill in my Vat stuff. Yes, I could do it myself but I've got better things to do, like watch football. All I'm doing, it seems to me, is collecting tax for the government. I charge other people Vat, count it up, then hand it all over. Ray gave me a headache just mentioning the subject.

Later that day, he sent me a fax with some Vat stuff on it—and blow me, he seemed to be right. Something called a flat-rate scheme for small businesses had come in while I wasn't watching. I rang the Vat people and spoke to a bloke who said, yeah, I'll send you the stuff.

I now have notice 733—hurry, hurry and get your own copy. It lists all the various trades and professions that are entitled to pay Vat at a flat rate, some as low as 5%. I couldn't believe it. If I was running my own newsagents, that's all I would pay. Publicans pay 6%; printers 8.5%; photographers 10%. Journalists are there, as Ray had said, at 12%.

I'm not actually a journalist, not any more. In real life I'm an author, as is my wife. Author wasn't listed, so I rang the Vat man again. It was found under 'any activity not elsewhere specified'—and I need pay only 11%, even better than Ray. I then rang my accountant and shouted at him: why hadn't he told me about this new scheme? He said it was in a letter, sent out by his firm last year. That was true, but it didn't explain it, or give any details. I assumed it must just be a different way of paying the same old amounts. As I understand it, I'll still charge Vat at 17.5%, but will pay a flat 11% of my total turnover to the Vat people.

The downside is that you cannot any more claim back Vat paid on work-related things you may have bought. In my case, these are piddling, so I should still gain quite a bit of money. And there will be far less paperwork, with no need to record all the individual details. Well done the Vat people: at long last an attempt to simplify a stupid system. And thanks, Ray. Sometimes it does pay to have friends.

The Reverand Vertrue Sharp, preacher, teacher, hay and cattle raiser, left his $2 million estate to a range of charities and a local children's hospital in Tennessee. During his lifetime he knew how to make the pennies count. Press reports said he refused to buy coffee at a favourite restaurant after the price was hiked to 75 cents—buying it elsewhere instead at a third of the cost. He also refused to buy paper towels, considering them an extravagance. Sharp died in 1999, aged 94.

THOROUGHLY MODERN ME

— £ —

Living in modern times is so expensive. I don't mean the obvious things that now carry obscene price tags, such as houses or a match programme at Spurs. I am talking about the objects we need to acquire in order to demonstrate, if only to ourselves, that we live in modern times. As I look round my room where I am penning these words, sorry personally computing them, I am rather proud of the fact that I am bang up to date, thanks to a visit yesterday to Argos.

Unlike my dear wife. At this moment, she's upstairs in her little room shifting words with a fountain pen and ink. That's the full extent of her technology. She won't even answer the phone. I have to do it, then shout for her. I suspect this dates back to her father, who never had a phone in their house in Carlisle. In emergencies, they went to the box on the corner. She had to go in and make the call while her dad would wait and 'keep watch'. She never did discover what he was looking out for.

I have a system for buying new technology. I wait for two years after it has come on the market to see if it really might have some sort of working life — and if it has fallen in price. Hence my trip to Argos last week. It was my second visit in a year, yet surprisingly nobody recognised me or shouted 'stand by the tills, here comes the big spender'. I went on a mad spree and bought a digital camera.

My old 35mm steam camera, a Canon Sure Shot, has not recovered since I dropped it after my third mojito in a beach caff in Bequia. Should I buy a similar one, and go backwards in time, or get one of these new-fangled digital things? Even the poorest people have them. Michael at my local chemist, where I get my steam snaps developed, shook his head and explained that people don't realise the extra expense of digital cameras, such as the ink and the special paper, not to mention a memory card, whatever that is.

My son got a £300 digital camera two years ago. Last time I looked they had come down to £200. Still too much for me. Then on the bus last week I picked up an Argos leaflet someone had left behind that said 'WOW! 3.2m pixel digital camera for only £79.99'. I didn't even stop to work out what pixies have got to do with it, though at Argos they do have lots of strange lifeforms lurking round the back.

I have even managed to print out my first digital picture on ordinary cheap copy paper. It happens to be a shot of my fireplace, which was where my camera was pointing at the time. It is very blurry and you need to be told in advance that it is a fireplace. But I think it's amazing. My modern life is complete.

Over there is my mobile phone. Nobody can say I'm out of touch, even though I haven't used it for a year. My computer gleams, and no wonder. A year old, but still brand new. I will keep writing on my Amstrad PCW9512 until it packs up. The Amstrad is still my No1 modern device, even though nobody else considers it modern because it's about 15 years old and has 3m words on the clock. Second fave is my fax machine. I'd be lost without it. Third is the video recorder. I held out for years, saying they were stupid. TV is mostly rubbish, so who wants to record rubbish? Then in came wall-to-wall live football and even I can't watch more than three games a day.

My fourth favourite is my photocopier, so handy when you work from home. Fifth is my video camera. I was in love with my Super 8 silent thing for decades but camcorders are brilliant: cheap and easy to use.

My wife enjoys it when there's an electricity cut. She can hear me screaming while she quietly pens away but she is missing out on so many of our modern-day pleasures.

Then going round my room, I found this ugly shiny round thing in a corner — a CD player, covered in dust. I bought it cheap, two years ago, feeling I should have one. I never got round to buying any CDs and now it is probably about to become obsolete. If digital cameras become prehistoric in two years' time, I'll be spitting. But at £79.99, I'm in the modern world — for this week anyway.

> "The difference between a debit card and a credit card is that a debit card spends money you haven't got now and a credit card spends money you haven't got later."
>
> — Guy Browning, *The Guardian Weekly*, 30 October 2004

RURAL RIDES

— £ —

We had gone for a walk round Derwent Water, my wife, daughter and granddaughter Ruby, and were about to catch the launch across the lake to Keswick from Nicol End when it started chucking it down. I always say there is no such thing as bad weather in Lakeland, only bad clothing—and it's true. We had flimsy, skimpy rain-wear, as it had been such a warm day, so we were soon soaked through. We all rushed for the boat when it arrived only to be told it was going round the lake.

It was not the one we were waiting for, to take us one stop straight across to Keswick. It would be £15 to go round the lake, instead of £3 for a single stop.

"Hmm, I think we should wait for the next one," I said.

"You mean beggar," yelled my wife. "Can't you see we're all absolutely sodden and Ruby is shivering."

"We'll only have to wait a minute or so," I bleated.

"Well, we're getting on now, out of the rain, however much it costs. It's only money."

So we all did. Naturally, by the time we got to Keswick, the sun had come out and we were feeling more cheerful, apart from me. I was still thinking about the £15 I'd had to spend.

I had parked in Keswick in the car park beside the theatre. It had been full, the day being so hot, so I had been forced to park on a piece of grass, not in a proper bay, but I had paid for a parking ticket, for all of £2.80. God, the cost of parking today. My wife got to the car first to find a bit of plastic rubbish sticking to the screen. I'd been fined £60. I started shouting 'Bloody hell, bloody hell', which of course Ruby (aged four) immediately copied. My wife, meanwhile, was smiling.

"It's not funny," I said. "Just don't say anything."

"It's only money," she repeated.

"Not that again," I replied.

"But it is. You can afford it. You're not on the poverty line. We won't starve. Thank your lucky stars that you can manage it. Just pay it and move on."

I did pay it, over the phone, by Visa, having checked the small print first to see that by paying promptly the fine would come down to £30. But I can't forget. It's ingrained; it's in the blood. I can pay ordinary bills easily, and buy quite expensive stuff, especially if it's for my collections. And I have given lots away. But it's having to pay extra, like the £15 for the boat, or that stupid parking fine, that unsettles me. I suppose it's the waste, the extra pointless forking out, for no return, no gain, no pleasure — especially when it happens to be due in some way to my own daftness.

"But at your age, you should have risen above it," said my wife, when hours later she could sense me still seething. "Do get things in proportion. God knows, there are more important things to worry about in the world than a parking fine."

How true, how very true, you are so wise, but put a sock in it, eh? If I want banal advice, I'll buy some Christmas crackers.

Three days later, by which time our daughter and Ruby had returned to London, I was beginning to move on. But then I decided to look again at the parking fine notice, to see if there was a loophole. Perhaps they had got my car registration wrong, or the time. But I couldn't find the notice anywhere.

"It's in Ruby's scrap book," said my wife. It had been stuck in, along with things like the Derwent Water boat leaflets, tickets for a sheep show, postcards, a scrap of wool and leaves from my orchard — all highlights of her hols in Lakeland.

Sir Nathan Meyer, the first Lord Rothschild, was alighting from a London hansom cab one evening and gave the driver a pretty measly tip.

"Your Lordship's son gives me a great deal more than this," commented the driver.

"I daresay he does, said Lord Rothschild. "But then he's got a rich father. I haven't."

WONDERFUL WILKOS

— £ —

Is being mean expensive? Does it turn out costly to be canny? We have these ongoing philosophical discussions all the time in our house, especially today when I came home from Carlisle with a whole load of cheap stuff from Wilkinson. It appears to be a hardware store, but as I wandered round, getting more and more excited, I came across stationery, gardening equipment, pharmacy things, food, sweets, toys, items I didn't know I wanted—until I saw the low prices.

Wilkinson has usurped Staples to become my favourite shop. I always imagined it was peculiar to

Carlisle but I discover it began in Leicester in the 1930s and is now nation-wide, with 235 shops. But it's still a private family firm.

I bought two sticks of deodorant in my excitement. My wife said, ugh, horrible stuff, you don't even use deodorant. That's true, I said, but they were two for £1. How could I resist? And that's the first moral in this little tale. Mean people buy unnecessary things, just because they are bargains. I also picked up a large box of grass seed for only £2.99, about a quarter of the price of the grass I'd recently bought in an old-fashioned hardware store in Keswick. I will use it some day but I have to admit I don't actually need any now. Then I got three ring binders at 59p each. Come on, have you ever seen them priced so low?

Now I do use binders, all the time, for my many collections and treasures, so she couldn't criticise that as an impulse or pointless purchase. But when I got home, guess what? I already had 10 cheap binders, still shrink-wrapped, at bargain, sale or closing-down prices ranging from 99p to £1.99. I'm praying for a world shortage of ring binders, then I'll have cornered the market. Meanwhile, I dread going into some even cheaper shops and finding them at 39p.

I blame my parents. No, sorry, growing up in the war. Deodorant didn't exist and we ate sawdust, thinking it was bananas.

My dear wife rightly points out that such searching

and falling for bargains often works out more expensive because you buy stuff you wouldn't otherwise need or know about. And chances are that the quality will not be as good, so you will also lose. I deny this. Wilkinson has pretty decent stuff. Then there's the stress and strain, so she alleges. I do dither, ponder and frown, for she has caught sight of me across a crowded supermarket. I tell her she's mistaken: that's how I look when I'm enjoying myself. It's a state of bliss.

My wife decides what she needs and can afford. She then buys it, at the first place, the first shelf, without looking for alternatives, often without knowing the price. Then it's straight out, to get on with more important things, such as living. She is disturbed by the phenomenon of 'buy one, get one free'. They are magic words to me but they knock her off her moral balance. She might want the thing anyway, but only one, thank you. She doesn't want any extra, not even for free. Yet at the counter, if the assistant points out she is due a free extra one, she will smile sweetly and accept, if only because it would look snooty to decline.

Then she comes home, unsettled, discomfited, especially when I pounce on the shopping and say, ah ha, buying bargains, are we?

*Top money terms in the UK according
to a Barclays Bank report*:

1. *Dosh*
2. *Dough* (popular in Scotland)
3. *Readies* (used in Wales)
4. *Brass* (popular in the north west and Yorkshire)
5. *Bread* (common in the north east)
6. *Wad* (a favourite in the West Midlands)
7. *Lolly* (popular in the West Country)
8. *Wedge*
9. *Wonga* (top slang term in London)
10. *Moolah* (a southern favourite)

Money terms no longer in use or less common today:

1900s *Mazuma*
1910s *Scratch*
1920s *Lettuce*
1930s *Bread*
1940s *Lolly*
1950s *A bomb*

I'M HOPING TO CASH IN ON
MY LOUSY PARKING

— £ —

My lunch break last Monday cost £335.30. A hell of a lot, considering I only had coffee, a ham and cheese toastie and a swim—a total of £6.30. If life is what happens when you are busy making other plans, so is expense. It hits you just when you least expect it.

I was parking the car at Sainsbury's in Cockermouth, leaving my wife to do the shopping, about to go off for my swim and snack. It was very busy for a Monday but then shopping is the national pastime. I saw a gap at last and a bloke standing beside it. I asked if he was keeping it. He said no, so I slowly drove in, making sure I didn't run over his toe. I felt the vaguest movement as my bumper slid along the side of the car to my left, but I just smiled, idiotically. Bad parker, eh? The bloke then went potty. I thought for a moment I had hit his toe. It turned out the car I had ever so slightly grazed was his. I got out and could hardly see the scratch but I mumbled an apology:

"Modern life, just look at my car, the scratches people have given me."

My car is so perforated and pitted it looks like a close-up of the moon.

"It's just a little scratch," I said. "It'll rub out with a damp rag."

He told me I had dented the door and the wing.

"It's going to cost you. What's your name, address and insurance company?"

I'm quite good on my own name and address, taking it slowly, but my insurance company, God knows.

I had my swim, and my snack, and had almost forgotten the little incident, thinking he would calm down. Surely nobody can get fussed over a small scratch on an old Golf? Later that day he rang to say he had been given an estimate of £329.

"Bloody hell," I said. "For that old car?"

"Do you mind?" he said. "It's an Alfa Romeo, just two years old and immaculate."

Shows how observant I am—almost as sharp as my parking. I dug out my insurance policy, with Norwich Union, to find out my position.

It took hours, perhaps days, going through automated helplines, whose main purpose seemed to be to help themselves—telling me my call would be monitored for training purposes, help improve their services, blah blah, and my details might be passed on to associated companies to help them, blah blah. I was screaming by the end. I've got too much work to do to waste time listening to stupid recorded voices. I eventually got through to a human who was very helpful. The company would take over the paperwork and if I didn't do it again in the next year, I wouldn't actually have to pay anything.

As for the £329, that was nothing for a scratch in a car park. The average is nearer £500. But what about the damage to my car? My car? I had in fact not even looked. No point, really. How could I recognise a new bump from an old one? Then the other bloke's insurance company, Churchill, started sending me letters, which was annoying. I think that's the worst aspect of these minor incidents: the time and paperwork it takes.

But some good, perhaps even some money, may come out of all this. I listened to so many stupid helplines all week that I decided to work on my own specially taped message. I tried it out first on Norwich Union.

"My name is Jo," said a nice voice from the Newcastle call centre. "How can I help you?"

"Before we continue, Jo." I said. "I have to tell you that I am monitoring this call. Any information you give me that proves unhelpful, not to say wrong and expensive, might be used as evidence in any forthcoming claims for damages or any legal action I may take. I might also pass on your name and number to thousands of time wasters who may approach you about double-glazing or Viagra. Oh, and I forgot to ask your mother's maiden name, date of birth, password, favourite football team..."

There was a long pause, then she started laughing.

"I'm not bothered. I know that all the information I'll give you is correct," she said.

Hmm, so I haven't got the wording quite right yet but I'm sure there's a market for customised tape messages. Then I might make some money out of my lunch break.

Slang terms for pound:

Nicker – in use from the early 1900s in London, may come from use of nickel to mint coins, or from the American nickel meaning 5 cents.

Quid – in the late 1600s it meant a guinea and in the 1700s a pound. May come from the Latin phrase 'quid pro quo', meaning something given in exchange for something else. UK bank notes still bear the words "I promise to pay the bearer…" as signed by the Chief Cashier at the Bank of England.

Maggie – referred to the new pound coin introduced in the 1980s which was, 'brassy, two-faced and thinks it's a sovereign' —like the prime minister of the time, Margaret Thatcher.

BARGAIN ALTAR BREAD WON'T
NOURISH MY SOUL

— £ —

I was delivering the newspapers on Saturday for the last time before we return to London from Lakeland. I take turns when we live up here, taking them round our little valley. It was my first ever job. I didn't think I'd still be at it 50 years later.

Saturday is my day, which means I get to read the *Church Times*. In it I noticed this advert: 'Save up to 30% on altar bread!' I thought, I'll have some of that, sounds a bargain. Then came my second thought. How do I know it's a bargain, when I've never bought any altar bread? Double glaziers do this all the time: promise 30% off, but don't reveal any prices. Then came my third thought—don't be stupid, Hunt.

But altar bread is not what I'm on about. It's pensions. No, please, don't rush on to look for more awfully amusing quotes about money. I've just got a good advance on a book, my first income for three months. So I can now do what my accountant always advises—put the maximum allowed into my pension.

"You know it makes sense," he says, his mind already on the golf course.

But of course it's not sense. It's nonsense. I contact Prudential, Standard Life, Legal & General and various others, as I do every year, trying to work out the best annuity rate for a gent of my mature years, then bung them a large sum and immediately start taking it out again. Is that potty or what? I get 25% of my own money back in cash, and the rest becomes a piddling annual income, on which I pay higher-rate tax. Gawd, the paperwork this entails, the phone calls, the financial advisers (because most pension institutions won't deal direct with ordinary humans). Then, of course, each year the rules change. I've lost all that time, faffing about, so what's the point? Just to save a few quid. I no longer want to save the odd quid—an awful realisation. I want an easy, faff-free, paper-free, accountant-free and tax-man-free life.

For years I have glanced through all the Money pages, marking the choicer, sexier adverts, you know, the ones with pouting percentage points, half-naked annual rates. I go phew, look as this, pet, if I move our wad from Bristol & West to Northern Rock and leave it in for five years, thanks to the introductory bonus, their special loyalty rate, plus extra for not smoking or swearing, we'll end up with, let me see, £19.98 a year.

I have done this for years, moved stuff, just because I've spotted some chancer offering another 0.25 percentage points. What a waste of energy. I suppose it's okay if you have nothing else in your life, and you enjoy it, as many people do.

I met an elderly widow on a plane the other day who was a real whizz, knew every rate from every company. Each week she moves her few pounds round. But she has no other income, so an extra £19.98 a year matters.

Anyway, I've decided, at long last, no longer to put money in a pension scheme. It's not worth it for the faff—or the money. I am still working and hope to for some time. When I go I'd like to be found slumped over my hot Amstrad PCW, my finger on the 'exit' key. Until then, it's National Savings. Bugger the poor rates. And forget the bargain altar bread. Who needs it?

Canny famous people — supposedly:

Tommy Cooper – cabbies that drove Cooper could look forward to a teabag slipped into the pocket with the advice, "Get yourself a drink, mate."

The Queen – The Queen's staff are instructed to darn old dusters so they can still be used; turn worn double sheets into singles; and iron and re-use wrapping paper.

Michael Winner – Winner cuts his toothpaste tubes in half to get every last drop.

I WISH I'D HAD THE VISION TO
BECOME A TOP OPTICIAN

— £ —

If I was starting again now, what would I do to make money? I used to think of a nice little franchise, cashing in on the success of some international firm with a household name, such as McDonald's.

Last week I went into McDonald's in Hampstead High Street, which I do about once a week in this cold weather, after I've had my walk on the heath. But I don't go to eat, certainly not. I go to use the lavatory. It's always so clean, it's a joy to take advantage. Usually the restaurant is so busy that nobody notices you have just walked in off the street. But last Thursday afternoon it was empty. The staff were just hanging around, waiting for customers. Even I didn't have the cheek to use the lav. So I carried on, crossing my legs till I got home. Does that mean they're not making much money any more? Anyone with a McDonald's franchise must have cause for concern.

Kall Kwik, now I always thought that must be a nice little franchise. I do like anything to do with printing, but new technology is coming in all the time and people can do more at home on their own computers. Franchises do reflect fashions and changes. So perhaps it's not the easiest way to make money.

Plumbers can make a fortune, about £50,000 a year in London, and are always in demand. But I still don't understand the time-switch on our boiler and we've had it three years. Anyway, there's a huge waiting list for plumbing courses. Unless you've got a first in philosophy at Oxford you have no chance of being accepted. So that's out.

Dentists make a fortune — don't lie, we all know that. You now have to beg to be taken on, or queue up for days as they did recently in Scarborough. But I'd hate to be a dentist, staring into people's mouths all day. Ugh. Also, their assistants wear so much make-up. And they're always leaving.

Estate agents do well, taking a massive percentage of other people's wealth for very little work. All they need is an expensive-looking shirt, braces optional, clean fingernails and an ability to walk very quickly when chatting on a mobile phone. But there are now so many of them. In social esteem, they are on a par with journalists and politicians.

One of the current growth areas is selling stuff on Ebay. You go into second hand or collectors' shops these days, if you can catch them open, and they are even more superior and offhand than ever. They've lost interest in meeting human beings face to face. Now they can stay at home and flog their stuff via their computers for higher prices. With my 20 or so different collections, I'm always buying more rubbish, I mean treasures. The trouble is that on the rare occasions I've tried to sell, I got less than I paid for them. Not that I can remember what I paid. Also, I don't actually know what Ebay is.

As I was walking home, I saw a sign saying Denial Surgery. Goodness, these Hampstead shrinks are clever. They can now perform operations on people suffering from denial symptoms—and probably depression and compulsive disorders as well. When I got closer, I saw the sign said Dental Surgery. I realised I should have my eyes tested, so I started looking out for opticians and discovered a strange thing. I passed three that I swear were not there last time I looked and they are all enormous. You could have held a five-a-side football match in one of them. It must mean they are awash with money, able to lash out on massive premises for no real reason. A look at their prices will confirm this—hundreds of pounds for a bit of glass and wire that must cost only a few pennies.

So that's it. When I come back in another life, I plan to be an optician. Clean job, socially acceptable and while waiting for customers, you can play football.

"Lack of money is the root of all evil."
– George Bernard Shaw

"The holy passion of friendship is so sweet and steady and loyal and enduring in nature it will last a whole lifetime, if not asked to lend money." – Mark Twain

---

I'VE BEEN COPYING MY WIFE

— £ —

Women are supposed to do it all the time, so I've heard. They go out to buy a frock or a pair of shoes, and come back with stuff they didn't really want, but had to get. They then shove it at the back of the wardrobe, hoping to hide it at the back of their mind. Couldn't happen to me, could it? Why would I want to go out and buy clothes? I have clothes. I am sitting here typing, fully clothed. So obviously I don't need to buy any more. But, dear God, it's happening to me in another area, one in which I am not the slightest bit interested and one I hate, just hate, spending money on.

I have a photocopier, right? Had one for two decades, not the same one, but every eight years or so it packs up and I get another, just the cheapest, simplest Canon copier. Actually, they are not cheap. Photocopiers, unlike TVs and videos and fax machines, have not come down in price in recent years.

It's my extravagance now that post offices are disappearing. It's also the only bit of office machinery in our house that my wife uses. She works with pen and ink, as nature intended but often comes into my office, knocking first of course, in order to copy a letter she has written or some pages from a book. I let her use my copier, and I don't even charge. My latest one packed up three weeks ago, so I rang Staples, a firm I have relied on for at least a decade, because its catalogue promises next-day delivery. I was told it would arrive in two days' time, so I stayed in all day, waiting, but nobody came. There was still no sign of it five days later, and so began two weeks of hell. I spent at least 40 minutes every day raging, trying to get through to them to find out what had gone wrong. Nobody answered the phones or replied to faxes and letters.

Eventually I did get through, screamed and shouted, and cancelled the order. I then regretted it because I couldn't find any other place that sold basic Canon copiers. Even Argos doesn't do them any more. Then I couldn't get through to Staples again to re-order the cancelled order. What have I done? All this energy, wasting it on such a stupid thing when I've got so much to do, such as, well, trying to watch eight football games at the same time on Sky. Now that is knackering. Then someone did ring from Staples, apologised for mucking me around, all to do with a new warehouse, blah blah. They suggested I try Office World, a company I had never heard of, which they have apparently bought. Office World was working properly and would do next-day delivery. They gave me a direct line, which was a relief, instead of those infuriating 0800 numbers.

A bloke at Office World said that, no, they didn't have

a Canon copier. What people now have, he said, is an all-in-one printer, fax, scanner and copier. But I don't want that, I said. I have a fax already and a printer. I don't want a scanner, I'm not a doctor. I just want a simple copier, as I always have. I was about to hang up when he said they had a special offer on an all-in-one thingy, a Hewlett Packard, only £199, which they could deliver to me tomorrow. The minute I heard the words 'Okay then' trickling from my lips I knew I'd regret it. Yet I went ahead. What is wrong with me? But having expended so much time and energy, I just had to have something, anything, to show for it. It's the silly shopping syndrome. If you go shopping, you need to return with shopping, however silly.

It took me three hours to unpack it, set it up and work out the instructions. It's huge, hideous. The keyboard has 40 buttons and knobs and it's so complicated I'm sure flying a plane would be easier. It's also slower than my old one and makes a horrible noise. My dear wife, who doesn't know it has arrived yet, will never cope, and she'll mock me, the person who is supposedly so careful with money, for splashing out on something I didn't want and don't need. I know, the back of my wardrobe. If I put it there now, she'll never find out. And, after all, it's not really all that far to the post office.

Two weeks later I got a call from Peter Birks, MD of Viking Direct, one of the world's biggest suppliers of office products, saying he had managed to track down a Canon copier, like the one I had, now discontinued. Would I like it, as a present, on behalf of the office supplies industry? So what did I say. Yes, of course. So now we have two. I think I'll open a proper office.

MONEY CAN BUY HAPPINESS BUT IT CAN'T FIX BOILERS

— £ —

It's brilliant having money. I am so lucky because I have loads of it and think nothing of buying an evening paper, even when I haven't finished the morning one or ordering a cappuccino when I know a cup of tea is miles cheaper.

I count my blessings all the time, because money does solve problems in life. It takes away the anguish, the waiting. Everyone knows that, especially people with no money. Poor sods. How do they cope? Take private medicine. I've never actually gone private before and I don't have medical insurance. But I have arthritis, doctor, which has been giving me gyp for about a decade. The rheumatology experts at the Royal Free Hospital have been very good, filling me full of lovely drugs but I think the left knee is now a goner and will probably have to be replaced.

So I needed to see a knee expert, which I was told could take months on the NHS. I just wanted some quick advice — am I at that stage or not — so I thought, dammit, I'll go private. I can afford it. It's brilliant having money. I got the top knee man recommended and a letter was written to him on October 22.

I was told it would cost me £160 for the consultation. Piddling money for someone as rich as me. Would hardly get you lunch for two in the West End or one seat for a game at Arsenal's new stadium. I sat by the phone all week, waiting for the call. Hiya Hunt, glad you can join us, come round as quickly as possible — oh, and don't forget to bring your knee. Silence for a week, then a month, then another month. I have finally got an appointment: for December 22. Call that queue jumping? Sounds like queue crawling to me.

Oh, there were reasons: the appointment letter was sent by mistake to my GP, not my home, and it just lay there. All the same, I thought that money was meant to ensure efficiency, get you ahead of the herd. OK then, take British Gas. For three weeks now our boiler has been breaking down. In this case, I do have cover, three-star something, had it for 10 years. I have to praise British Gas for sending blokes out when I ring the 0845 number. In fact, we've had six engineers calling. They have put in endless new parts but the problem is still there.

It won't start in the morning, so we come down in freezing cold. It has taken us back to our childhood in Carlisle in the 1940s and 1950s when you were scared to get out of bed in the morning in case your bare feet froze on the lino. Our dear children can't share those heart-breaking memories. Like most of today's spoilt modern people, they have always known central heating. It was thought at first we needed something called Powerflush to take any sludge out of the water. This turned out to be an extra, not covered by three star — they're not stupid. The engineer gave me a printed-out estimate of £464.99 (I did like that exact price) which I signed.

One interesting thing about modern gas engineers — and we are now on first name terms with loads, one of whom lives in Liverpool but helps out poor Londoners — is their posh, blue tool bags. They zip them open with a flourish to reveal a laptop and printer. Ever so dinky and high-tech. I'm also amazed by their attitude to parking fines. Our street has parking restrictions between 10am and noon, so I offered them some of my resident's passes. But they said: "Nah, I won't be paying, squire."

Anyway, I faxed a copy of the estimate the same day, with a covering letter saying urgent, old bloke with dodgy knee, please be kind. Silence for two weeks. I couldn't actually get a direct phone number. Every time I rang one of those stupid 0845 numbers I was told they didn't have it, but the next engineer would tell me. When he came, he said oh no, I only have an internal number on my mobile. So, while we still wait for the boiler to be mended I have thought of a good way of using my untold wealth. I am offering £10 to the first person to give me a direct phone number for British Gas engineers. See, money does have its uses.

Igor Stravinsky, the Russian-born composer who became an American citizen, got into an argument with an airport official about a charge for his excess baggage. The official, very patiently, explained the reasons, saying that if everyone took as much as they liked on a plane, the plane wouldn't fly.

"It's not the logic I am objecting to." said Stravinsky. "It's the money."

UP TO MY KNEES IN HOLIDAY COSTS

— £ —

This morning, all being well, touch wood, my dear wife and I will be on our way to the Bahamas. It's our annual summer hols, which we always have at this time.

I've been examining my bank balance constantly because a monster tax bill has to be paid while I'm away. I'm still juggling to make sure there will be enough on the right day to cover it. Naturally, I don't want to send the cheque in advance. Why should the taxman get to play with my money?

My bank balance has just had an unexpected dent made in it. I want to be fit and well on my hols and standing at the bar holding rum punches can be very tiring. I went to see a private consultant about my dodgy knee and he charged me £160. He then recommended a physio called Mr McCoole. His fee was £45 for half an hour. He recommended arch supports, sort of little inner soles to put in your shoes. They look like flimsy bits of plastic but they cost £23.50. I nearly fell over. And on my poorly knee. Then he said I really should have Birkenstock sandals for the beach, not my cheapo street-market ones that cost £10.

I trailed down to Covent Garden and bought a pair at

£69. I can't believe I did that. But they are billed as vegetarian sandals. If we get hungry in the Bahamas we can always eat them. So far, taking my knee to the Caribbean has cost £297.50. On the other hand, I've just totted up our annual Premium Bond wins, £1,750, as I do at this time of year. I know the prizes add up to only a 3.2% return—but it is tax-free.

Then it was time for travel insurance. Because my wife and I are now over 65, they expect you not to go on hols ever again, but stay at home in bed, the bastards.

My daughter, who went to Lapland over Christmas with Ruby, found the Post Office's deal was the best. But guess what they quoted my wife and I for three weeks— £438 or £569 for an annual deal. You can get whole holidays cheaper than that. You'd expect Saga to be kind to oldies but they don't even offer annual insurance, and quoted £186 for three weeks. The best annual deal I've found is Admiral at £192. I'll probably take that.

There's a couple of other things that I've decided to take on my hols. First, a little hot water bottle, as used by children. I find this awfully efficacious when I get earache. I'm also taking a freezer thing, the sort you keep in a fridge and then stick round a bottle of white wine to get it cool quickly. I find they are excellent for inflamed joints during an arthritis attack. Just a couple of medical tips I'd like to pass on. Both of these have cost me nothing, because I've had them in the house for ages. See, you don't have to spend a fortune to go on holiday.

"People who change trends make money."
– David Yelland, ex-editor of *The Sun*

"Select stocks the way porcupines make love
— very carefully."
– Bob Dinda, banker

THE MONEY DOCTOR
WILL SEE YOU NOW

— £ —

Money can make you ill. It's now reaching epidemic proportions all over the western world, yet so many of the disorders have not been properly understood. I have the honour of being visiting professor earnmeritus at the department of financial medicine at the University of Carlisle. In layman's terms, I will describe some of the more common complaints.

Premiumbonditis: the symptoms to look out for are hands shaking and lips quivering with excitement whenever a neat white envelope arrives that you can clearly see has come from Glasgow. Patients should sit down and stay calm. You know you're not a winner. It's more than likely to be from your old Aunt Isa in Cambuslang, late with her Christmas card.

Repetitive share syndrome: despite all advice, all experience, all common sense, you keep buying stupid shares in the hope that some day soon even stupid shares will rocket.

Brown's disease: a tendency to scream and shout, kick the wall, whenever the chancellor uses the word 'prudence'.

Peptic ulcers: a nasty feeling in the gut, which can arrive suddenly when you are looking in a drawer for an old mint and you come across those rubbish Peps you bought years ago. Close the drawer quickly, nail it up, lie down in a darkened room.

ATM addiction: the symptoms here are mental, not physical. You know there is absolutely no point in returning to the cash machine to check your latest ministatement. You did it 10 minutes ago, and 10 minutes before that, when you know there's no chance of money suddenly appearing from nowhere. Do get a grip.

Irritable bank syndrome: the desire to murder someone when you see the queue stretching right to the door and at the front some eejit is paying in his dodgy takings in tuppenny bits.

Ninety-nine uses for a dead Vat inspector: oops, sorry, wrong list.

Compulsive annuity disorder: checking the annuity rates every week, yet putting off the decision to cash in your pension, take the money and, well, die. You are suffering from two delusions: rates are bound to improve, and you might never die.

Suntimeswealthosis: this eats into the soul and can utterly destroy even the most well balanced. It strikes the moment you read *The Sunday Times* Rich List of all those lucky sods, not half as clever as you, who have somehow amassed millions. Fortunately, it strikes only once a year.

Equitable swine fever: mainly attacked middle classes, bringing many to their knees. Caused by those swines at the Equitable Life Assurance Society.

IFA dependency: a mental delusion that is very hard to throw off. Suckers, sorry sufferers, believe that independent financial advisers somehow know what they are doing, they will help you and that there is nothing in it for them. When you feel such fantasies coming on, just ask yourself— if they were the slightest bit smart, they'd be in Barbados, not coming to your house and wasting your time with a load of nonsense you don't even understand.

Chronic Brownenvelopeism: panic attacks can be caused by brown envelopes marked IR. Envelopes from Customs and Excise, parking authorities and your local council can also cause high blood pressure and mild hysteria.

Poverty: an infectious disease, caused by lack of money. Can be fatal.

"The greatest riches are ignorance of wealth."
– Oliver Goldsmith

"It takes a lot of money to lead a simple life."
– Johnny Depp

BUYING A BOND — ONE OF
MY MANY OWN GOALS

— £ —

Regrets—I've had a few, such as one that Northern Rock has just kindly brought to my attention. I had forgotten all about a guaranteed capital bond that I took out in July 1999. I'd remembered I'd bought something like that but I'd forgotten the details.

I've got so much on my mind at present, such as all the Euro 2004 wallcharts from every newspaper. It takes ages filling them in. So it was jolly good of Northern Rock to write and tell me the bond will mature on July 5. It's perfect timing for my whopping tax bill which is due at the end of next month. 'Please note,' the letter added, 'that if the FTSE100 is below the benchmark level on July 5, 2004, no interest will be payable.' Benchmark? Did they invest my money in a joinery firm? Had Northern Rock become a barrister's chambers? The letter is in very small print. I read it again and found that when I gave them my money to play with in July 1999, the Footsie was at 6,592. Now it's at 4,494.

Fat chance of it zooming up by nearly 50%—unless England had gone on to win Euro 2004, the country had gone delirious with joy and everyone had rushed out to put their worldly wealth into shares. So that was a mistake. But we all have similar regrets as we travel through life, about daft investments we can't believe we made, pension plans we stupidly bought. No, I'm not going to mention Equ—— again.

I also regret things I did not do. About 10 years ago I met someone selling a cup final programme for 1923, the first time it was held at Wembley, so it had great historic value. He wanted £100. I offered £90. Get lost, he said. A month later, I thought oh well, what's another tenner? I'll pay him his £100, greedy devil. And of course it had gone. Today they never come up for less than £1,000.

If you really, really want something and you can afford it, then pay the going rate. Wise words, Hunt. What a pity you always ignore them. We had a huge Sheila Fell painting, eight feet across, on our living room wall for years. It had a very small hole in one corner, made by our son Jake with his snooker cue. It wasn't his fault, he said — the snooker table was too small. We sold the painting 10 years ago at Sotheby's. I think we decided it was too big for that wall. We got £3,000, which was reasonable at the time. Later I saw it in pride of place at the Royal Academy. It must now be worth £50,000. And we could easily have found space for it.

There's this lovely house on Downshire Hill in Hampstead, London. Every time I pass it I have to cross the road and look the other way. I went to an auction about 20 years ago, when for a few weeks we were thinking about moving. Well, I was, though my wife had said, 'No chance'. I bid £32,000 for it and it went for £35,000. It must be worth £2m now.

And there are other houses all over London and the Lake District, not to mention the Algarve and Majorca. Shame I never got my chequebook out. But at least regretting things you never bought isn't as costly as the many you did.

Louis B. Meyer, the movie mogul, was being asked by a colleague to contribute to charity.

"You can't take it with you, you know," said the colleague.

"In that case," said Meyer, "I'm not going."

"Money is better than poverty,
if only for financial reasons."
– Woody Allen

"Money is a bad servant but a good master."
– 1633, Messinger in his book *New Way*

"Money often costs too much."
– Ralph Wold Emerson

DYING TO KNOW THE OUTCOME

— £ —

In Michael Holroyd's book Mosaic he describes how his wife, Margaret Drabble, is annoyed by some unhelpful letter from her publisher and exclaims:

"I wish I were dead." On hearing this pitiful wail, Michael cries out: "For God's sake don't say that—I couldn't cope with the paperwork."

I know how he feels, although in my case, it would be the other way round. I do all the paperwork in this house. My dear wife doesn't have to bother her pretty head, as long as she keeps earning, which is why I still have her feet nailed to her desk. She would be lumbered if I popped my clogs first.

But I think a far worse fate, and one my little mind contemplates more and more, is not the thought of dying and someone else having to sort out all the mess, but dying and not knowing the end of the story. I'd be really furious, for example, if I died and never knew whether Equitable Life ever paid back all the thousands I believe I am owed. Or whether the mad house prices kept going up and up, thus confounding all the clever experts.

More worrying is what's going to happen to the FTSE 100. I have invested two wads in five-year National

Savings guaranteed-equity bonds. The capital is safe, thank God, but any return depends on the growth in the index. I took out the first in April 2002 when the Footsie was at 5,220. It's due to mature in April 2007 and I can't see myself making much, if anything.

The second I started in April 2003 when the index was at 3,847. So surely I will get a decent return on April 9, 2008 when the bond matures? But say I died on April 8, 2008. I'd be so livid—not knowing what the final level was, or how much I'd made.

I've got similar index-related nonsenses that were all dreadful mistakes, because there was no guarantee that I would get back my capital. I even have rubbish tied to the Hang Song, the Ying Tang Yong and indexes in countries I've never heard of. I must have been potty. But I want to be here, alive and counting, when they mature, if only to burn the evidence of my foolishness.

Thinking these thoughts—which to me are not at all morbid, though my family tell me to shut up—has made me start putting money into investments where the capital and interest rate is guaranteed. So that means boring fixed-rate bonds with Northern Rock for one year or tax-free two-year certificates from National Savings. I should see them out, if I don't up the Beaujolais rate to more than a bottle a day.

I know I could get slightly better rates by shopping around at other building societies, but unless you are a member they all now insist on seeing your fingerprints, birth and swimming certificates, DNA, bus pass, etc. I rang to find out what was required at Leeds and Holbeck, why all this evidence of identity was needed. 'Money laundering,' said a voice. Oh, I replied, you do that as well, do you?

Of course, none of us wants to miss the good bits. We want to see our grandchildren grow up or at least get through some of the vital stages. And imagine being at the World Cup in 2006, with England and Brazil nil–nil with three minutes of extra time to go, then having a heart attack and never knowing the final score. Wouldn't that be a sickener?

One thing about money, now I've suddenly become boring and sensible, is that you can arrange it so you do know what happens next. All I have to do first is hang on until 2008.

"With enough inside information and a million dollars, you can go broke in a year."
– Warren Buffett

"The man who dies rich dies in disgrace."
– Andrew Carnegie

"Money never goes out of season."
– 1616, quoted by Draxe in his *Biblia Scholastica*

Nor does writing about money. We hopes.

RULE OF NIGHT by Trevor Hoyle
ISBN 1-904590-01-2 · £8.99

IF THE SIXTIES WERE SWINGING, THE SEVENTIES WERE THE HANG-over—darker, nastier, uglier—especially if you lived on a council estate in the north of England.

Rule of Night was first published in 1975 and has since become a cult classic. It pre-dates the current vogue for 'hard men' and 'football hoolie' books by 25 years.

It is, however, much more than this. Trevor Hoyle creates a chillingly detailed world, where teenagers prowl rainy fluorescent-lit streets dressed as their *Clockwork Orange* anti-heroes. The backdrop is provided by Ford Cortinas, Players No.6, the factory, the relentless struggle to maintain hope.

Hoyle, who has since been published by John Calder (home to Samuel Beckett and William S. Burroughs), has added a fascinating afterword to his original book which has been out of print and highly sought-after for many years.

. . .

THE FAN by Hunter Davies
ISBN 1-904590-02-0 · £9.99

HUNTER DAVIES IS ONE OF BRITAIN'S MOST ACCLAIMED WRITERS and journalists. He has written over 30 books, among them modern classics, *The Beatles* and *A Walk Around The Lakes*. *The Glory Game*, published in 1972, is a benchmark work on football and is still in print today.

The Fan is a collection of very personal, unusual pieces about his life as a supporter. He observes football in its sovereignty of the late 1900s and early 2000s and tackles the big topics of the day: Beckham's haircuts, high finance, the price of pies, the size of match day programmes, the enormous wages, the influence of Sky TV, England's numerous managers.

Along the way, he also lets us into his home life, in London and the Lake District, his family, his work, his tortoise, his poorly knee (caused by too much Sunday football).

Originally published in the *New Statesman* magazine, *The Fan* catches Davies at his very best and most amusing. It will appeal to supporters of any age, sex and loyalties.

L O V E   S O N G S by Crass

ISBN 1-904590-03-9 · £9.99

Our love of life is total,
everything we do is an expression of that.
Everything that we write is a love song.
— Penny Rimbaud, *Yes, Sir, I Will*

CRASS: A RURAL COLLECTIVE BASED IN ESSEX, FORMED IN 1977 OF A diverse and eclectic group of individuals who operated for several years using music, art, literature and film as vehicles to share information and ideas. They also wanted to change the world.

This is a collection of words spanning those seven short years; a book of shock slogans and mindless token tantrums. An anthology of passionate love songs that sought to inspire a generation, and succeeded.

. . .

S U M   T O T A L by Ray Gosling

ISBN 1-904590-05-5 · £9.99

SUM TOTAL IS A LOST MASTERPIECE OF BRITISH LITERATURE, a restless, hungry riposte to America's finest Beat writers.

Written in 1961 when he was just 21, Gosling's itchy 'sort of' autobiography is a startlingly original take on the England of the early Sixties: rock 'n' roll, trains, dead-end jobs, drizzle, hitchhiking, jukebox cafés, trudging through hometown streets.

All the time he remains gloriously indulgent, disillusioned yet hopeful, tired but desperate for every new day.

Although now famous for hundreds of television and radio documentaries, in *Sum Total* Gosling reveals himself as a writer years ahead of his time, presenting a skew-whiff, arch and droll view of the world, both inside and out.

He has added a typically idiosyncratic and lengthy preface to the original text.

DIARY OF A HYPERDREAMER
by Bill Nelson

ISBN 1-904590-06-3 · £9.99

BILL NELSON IS ONE OF BRITAIN'S MOST RESPECTED CREATIVE forces. He came to prominence in the Seventies with Be Bop Deluxe and later Red Noise. He has collaborated with like-minds such as Yellow Magic Orchestra, David Sylvian, Harold Budd and Roger Eno and still releases a prolific amount of new music.

Diary of a Hyperdreamer is his day-by-day journal in which he ponders on life, art and the nation. His unique perspective is fed by a career creating and producing music, photography, painting and video.

Written from his home in a hamlet in north Yorkshire, he also includes engaging details of his family life, regular musings on mortality, along with reflections on his childhood and former life as a globe-trotting 'pop star.'

· · ·

THE PRICE OF COAL by Barry Hines

ISBN 1-904590-08-x · £9.99

BARRY HINES IS A MASTER CRAFTSMAN. WHILE HE IS RIGHTLY celebrated for his classic, *A Kestrel for a Knave* (later filmed as *Kes*), his other work is equally powerful.

The Price of Coal is an uncompromising depiction of life at a colliery where beer, snooker, cricket and time spent on the allotment is the only respite from clawing coal from the earth.

A royal visit prompts the introduction of soft soap to the toilets, grass seeds scattered on the slag heap, and lashings of white paint across the site.

But when disaster strikes the superficial is forgotten as men fight for their lives in the darkness underneath collapsing seams of coal.

As ever, Hines proves himself an exemplary storyteller with a discerning eye for detail and when bolder, gaudier writing is long forgotten, his stays in the mind and nourishes it.

He has written a new foreword to the original text which was first published in 1979 and later adapted for television as two linked plays, directed by Ken Loach in the acclaimed *Play for Today* series.

LOOKS & SMILES by Barry Hines
ISBN 1-904590-09-8 · £9.99

LOOKS AND SMILES IS A LOST BULLETIN FROM THE EARLY-EIIGHTIES when the sun felt to have set permanently on hope and optimism. Unemployment was rampant, especially in the north where traditional industries were laid waste by Margaret Thatcher and her government.

Set amid this gloom, *Looks and Smiles* is an under-stated love affair between unemployed school-leaver Mick and Karen who works in a town centre shoe shop. They both want little more from life than a decent chance.

As ever, Hines proves himself an exemplary storyteller with a discerning eye for detail. He never resorts to sentimentality, and hope, however slender, flickers always.

The book was originally published in 1981 and later made into a film by Ken Loach.

. . .

KICKED INTO TOUCH (PLUS EXTRA-TIME)
by Fred Eyre
ISBN 1-904590-12-8 · £9.99

FRED EYRE'S SPORTING LIFE BEGAN FULL OF PROMISE WHEN he became Manchester City's first ever apprentice. He never made their first team. In fact, he seldom made anyone's first team. Injuries played a part but limited talent was the greater curse. As he plummeted down the leagues he had something few footballers possess: a stud-sharp memory and an ability to write humorously about the sport he loves.

Originally published in 1981, *Kicked Into Touch* has become an enigma —selling more than a million copies yet still retaining cult status within the sport and among fans. This new version has been completely revised, extended and updated with a new set of photographs included.

It is set to reach a new generation of football fans looking for an antidote to the glib reportage of a sport lost to show business.

ZONE OF THE INTERIOR by Clancy Sigal

ISBN 1-904590-10-1 · £9.99

'THE BOOK THEY DARED NOT PRINT', ZONE OF THE INTERIOR IS a lost classic of zonked-out, high-as-a-kite Sixties literature. It tells the story of Sid Bell, an American political fugitive in London, who falls under the spell of Dr. Willie Last (partly modelled on the radical 'anti-psychiatrist' RD Laing). This unlikely duo feast on LSD, mescaline, psilocybin and psycho-babble, believing that only by self-injecting themselves with schizophrenia will they become true existentialist guerrillas. Their 'purple haze' odyssey takes them into the eye of the hurricane — mental hospitals, secure units for the violent, the Harley Street cabal of the 'Sacred 7' and semi-derelict churches that come complete with an underground tank for the woman convinced she's a fish. Sigal's approach is richly sardonic and anti-establishment, of both right and left, in a jazz-influenced free-form prose, comic and serious, myth-puncturing and elegiac. Along the way Sigal, now an established Hollywood screen-writer, makes the case for a revolutionary period of mental health nursing whose task is as yet undone.

FORTHCOMING TITLES

CHRISTOPHER BARKER	*The Arms of the Infinite*	May 2006
HUNTER DAVIES	*The Second Half*	August 2006
ANDREW MARTIN	*Northside*	September 2006

more details: www.pomonauk.com

POMONA SOUNDS

POMONA SOUNDS IS OUR AFFILIATED RECORD LABEL.
The following CD albums are available on-line at :

www.pomonauk.com:

PS-001	The Rosenbergs *Ameripop*	£7
PS-002	Black September *Black September*	£10
PS-003	Mudskipper *Eggshells*	£10
PS-004	The Monkey Run *Escape From The Rake*	£10
PS-005	Crass *You'll Ruin It For Everyone*	£10
PS-006	Killing Stars *When The Light First Fell*	£10
PS-007	Black September *You Can Do Anything*	
	If You Set Your Mind To It	£10